TO EVERY THING, THER
IS A SEASON AND A TII
TO EVERY PURPOSE U
UNDER THE HEAVEN.
A TIME TO BORN AND

10

TO EVERY
IS A SEA
TO EVER
UNDER TIME HEAVEN.
A TIME TO BE BORN A

11

TO EVERY THING 1
THERE IS A SEASON
AND A TIME TO EVE
PURPOSE UNDER

12

To every thing there is a season
and a time to every purpose und
the heaven. A time to be born an
a time to die; a time to plant and
a time to pluck up that which is 1

13

To every thing there is
a season and a time to
every purpose under tl
heaven. A time to be bo

14

To every thing there is
a season and a time to e
every purpose under th
heaven. A time to be bor

15

TO EVERY THING THERE IS A SE
AND A TIME TO EVERY PURPOSE
UNDER THE HEAVEN · A TIME TO
BE BORN AND A TIME TO DIE; AT

16

To every thing there
is a season and a ti
to every purpose u
the heaven. A time 1

17

To every thing the
is a season and a t
to every purpose
under the heaven.

18

To every thing there is a season

and a time to every purpose una

the heaven. A time to be born ar

19

TO EVERY THING THERE I!
A SEASON AND A TIME TO
EVERY PURPOSE UNDER TI
HEAVEN · A TIME TO BE BO
AND A TIME TO DIE; A TIM

20

A Book of
Formal Scripts

ABCDEFGHIJKLMNOPQRSTUVWXYZ

WHAT SURVIVES IS ESSENCE IN TRADITION IT IS THE ESSENCE OF THE MILLENNIA SINCE LIFE CAME TO BE

CRAFT means cultivation of an intimacy with human life
a sympathy for all living things and creation,
and the realisation of the fundamental unity
of all aspects of life though diverse in form

FROM
CRAFTS & THE FUTURE
BY KAMALADEVI
CHATTOPADHYAH

Tradition is all pervasive and touches human life at every phase, it can never be broken~ Tradition is the seed from which life always blossoms

Gaynor Goffe
Craft (extracts from an article by Kamaladevi
Chattopadhyah). Various sizes of cursive italic minuscules
and capitals. Ink and gouache on paper. $27\frac{9}{16}'' \times 16\frac{3}{4}''$
(70 × 42.5 cm) 1988
(Crafts Council collection)

T·H·E M·U·S·E·U·M·S
FOUNDED 1889 · INCORPORATED 1930
A·S·S·O·C·I·A·T·I·O·N

This is to certify that

Brian R. Simpson

has been awarded the

F·E·L·L·O·W·S·H·I·P

of the Museums Association

in recognition of the

distinguished contribution

to museum development

A. President

PRESIDENT

John Woodcock
Certificate for the Museums Association. Humanist capitals and minuscules in black, the heading and flourishes (various letterforms for each of the series) in vermilion. Printed offset litho on Wiggins Teape Connoisseur paper. The name of the recipient subsequently written in vermilion gouache. The text was 'ranged left' for considerations of economy in the cost of writing names of recipients. A3 (420 × 297mm). 1988

A Book of
Formal
Scripts

JOHN WOODCOCK

with historical notes by
Stan Knight

A & C Black · London

First published 1992
A & C Black (Publishers) Limited
35 Bedford Row, London WC1R 4JH

ISBN 0–7136–3245–3

© 1992 A & C Black (Publishers) Limited

A CIP catalogue record for this book
is available from the British Library.

Typeset by August Filmsetting, St Helens
Printed in Great Britain by
BAS Printers Limited, Over Wallop, Hampshire

Contents

Entries in italic type denote pages devoted to historical exemplars.

Photographs

*from the Central Lettering Record

Introduction

This book is essentially a sequel to the article on 'Formal Scripts' in *The Calligrapher's Handbook* and to *Historical Scripts* by Stan Knight, both books published by A & C Black. The former was so constrained for space that, although it set forth a number of alphabets which might be thought of as the calligrapher's basic repertoire, it could not show them related to their historical origins.

The alphabets in this book include those from 'Formal Scripts', with some editing and extended comment, and a considerable number of others, whilst still deliberately remaining within the confines of formal alphabets written with the broad pen. All are paired with historical precedents which have separate notes about historical origins and techniques.

The book is meant for the students of calligraphy or serious amateurs who may already have begun short courses or attended workshops and who wish for guidance in extending their range of letterforms. It will also be useful to the beginner who finds difficulty in finding tuition other than from books, in which case it can be used in conjunction with *The Calligrapher's Handbook* which gives detailed information about materials.

The book does not include alphabets made with a brush or pointed, flexible pen, nor letters formed by the informal use of these tools nor by considerable manipulation of the broad pen nor by changes of pressure on the broad pen. This is not to denigrate the potential of such forms, but they are beyond the scope of this title. It can also be argued that a study of simply-made broad-pen forms is a good basis, if not the best, for an appreciation of letterform construction before any attempt at forms more dependent on manipulation or more natural to other tools. On the other hand, slight manipulation of the pen angle and some slight changes of pressure will often accompany a developing familiarity with an alphabet and the confidence which then allows it to be written at some speed, at which stage the wrist and finger movements natural to each individual will become apparent. These differences can be detected in some of the historical examples written at speed and are not to be confused with the deliberate changes of pen angle used to produce, for instance, the flat terminals to upright strokes of the Gothic Rotunda alphabet, or a consistency of thick or thin strokes throughout a roman alphabet.

General character and significant detail are the things to be sought, from whatever historical models one chooses to work. Where the best historical model is considered to be one previously featured in *Historical Scripts*, another page or section of a page of that manuscript has usually been illustrated here.

It should be pointed out that the order of the alphabets is not chronological, but the first part (up to page 35) is the suggested order of study.

The first part of the book covers alphabets which have become the common currency of our everyday reading and are in that sense 'basic'.

The second part covers alphabets which are more 'exotic' and will be of most use for the occasional expression of a particular mood, reference to history or perhaps as contrast to a texture of letters of a more anonymous sort.

The passages of text printed on the endpapers show each alphabet and indicate the sort of texture and rhythm of writing it can produce. It should be emphasised that they are only an indication of possibilities – these can be extended by changes of spacing and pen-weight. Subtle changes of skeleton form, serif or terminal formation will also add to the variety of possible developments from the model alphabets, which are themselves only a suggested starting point.

It is advisable to practise each alphabet (and it is important to start practising it in the form of words as soon as you feel able) until it can be written with some fluency and spontaneity. That is, until you feel unconstrained by having to stop and think about individual letter shapes. Then go on to the next alphabet, or develop variations on the one recently studied. It is not only the skeleton form and the way the particular weight and angle of pen flesh out that form which need to be learned. It is also the shapes of the counters which have to enter the memory bank, through practice, before concentration on the freedom proper to calligraphy can be achieved.

A note of caution should also be offered. In studying this extended range of exemplars, students may be tempted to try many or all at the expense of becoming proficient in a few. It has already been explained above that the first part of the book contains the 'basic repertoire'. Poorly conceived letterforms, even if written with an apparent verve or spontaneity, are a poor substitute for well-formed characters. The truly excellent piece of calligraphy depends on well-constructed letters first, then freedom of execution within a well-designed framework. To feel master of the range presented here, and minor variations of them, is sufficient task to represent for most people many years of study. Most calligraphic projects could be at least adequately carried out using the infinite permutations on two or three alphabets, and design variations suggested by the sense of the words being written. On the other hand, it is a pity not to consider the possibilities offered by the other alphabets here, and it is in this spirit that this volume is presented.

If a spontaneous piece of work is to be achieved, the simple practical business of choosing a pen (suitably sharp – or not so sharp according to the writing surface), well-adjusted reservoir (if one is to be used), nicely flowing ink

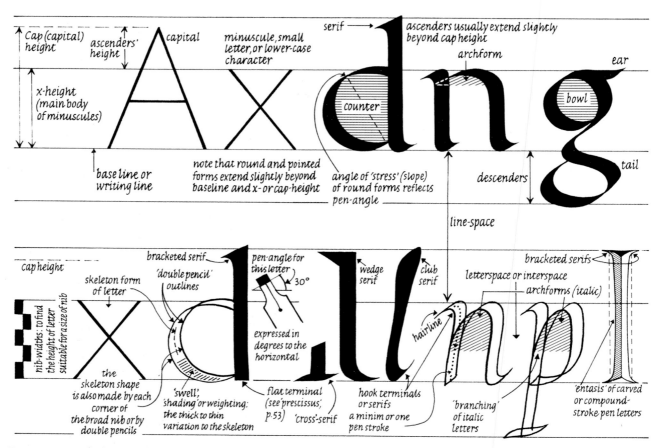

Intro:1 Parts of a letter and terms used in the text:
x-height, capitals (or caps), cap height, minuscules or lower case, ascender, descender, pen angle, archform, counter, serif, beaked serif, bowl, tail, terminal (without serif), hook terminal, skeleton, letter-space (inter-space).

or colour and the writing position must not be ignored. A pen held with the shaft almost vertical over a flat table will obviously allow the ink to drop quickly from the nib and to produce a blot. With a board at about 45° and the shaft of the pen more nearly horizontal, the ink flow is much reduced. Raising the board still further and lowering the pen shaft will slow down the ink flow until it stops altogether. Somewhere between the extremes will be a position which will suit the circumstances and it is important to get it right before embarking on the writing of any amount of text. A comfortable sitting position is also essential and the position of the writing line should be fixed at a level on the board that suits each person. Keeping this constant is very simply achieved by having a sheet of paper taped tightly across the board, its top edge just below this level, and placing the writing surface behind it (**Intro: 3**). The writing surface is then raised for each line to be written so that a constant pen angle is more easily achieved than if writing down a fixed page. In the latter case the angle of the writing arm to the horizontal would have to change during the progress down the page, and the pen angle with it, unless the writer were to resort to uncomfortable contortions.

Each alphabet in the book is preceded by a diagram of the letterform that indicates the weight, shown in terms of

nib-widths to the x-height, the required pen angle (variations will be noted where appropriate amongst the alphabet), the angle of the letters to the horizontal or vertical and the width of the basic **o**, and any other letter which is useful for comparison. Also included are thin diagonals which act as a reminder of the pen angle and counter(s) emphasised as solids (a reminder that it is as important to be aware of their shapes as of the positive letter shapes which are being written). These diagrammatic letters are shown in double outline (which can be thought of as the tracks left by the outer points of the broad nib). This can be produced by 'double pencils' — two pencils taped together. To produce a narrower 'pen-width' between the points the shaft of the pencils can be shaved down, or to make a wider 'pen-width' a slip of card can be inserted between the two (**Intro: 4**). Although this device does not make so obvious the weight of the letter and its relationship to the counter as do pen and ink, it has the advantage of making clear the construction — the almost architectural form — of the letter. It also shows how this is affected by pen lifts, the consequent joining of separate strokes or, alternatively, the continuous strokes linking parts of a letter; most importantly, perhaps, the way archforms join their uprights to give a strong form.

8

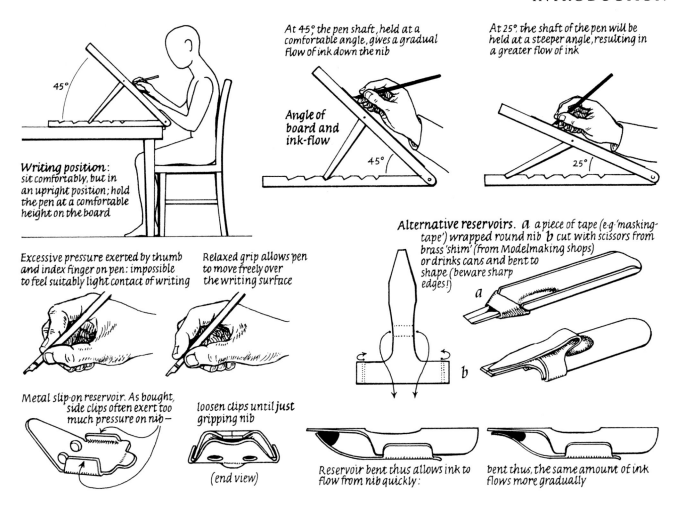

At 45° the pen shaft, held at a comfortable angle, gives a gradual flow of ink down the nib

At 25° the shaft of the pen will be held at a steeper angle, resulting in a greater flow of ink

45°

Writing position: sit comfortably, but in an upright position; hold the pen at a comfortable height on the board

Angle of board and ink-flow

45°

25°

Excessive pressure exerted by thumb and index finger on pen: impossible to feel suitably light contact of writing

Relaxed grip allows pen to move freely over the writing surface

Alternative reservoirs. *a* a piece of tape (e.g. 'masking-tape') wrapped round nib *b* cut with scissors from brass 'shim' (from Modelmaking shops) or drinks cans and bent to shape (beware sharp edges!)

a

b

Metal slip-on reservoir. As bought, side clips often exert too much pressure on nib —

loosen clips until **just** gripping nib

(end view)

Reservoir bent thus allows ink to flow from nib quickly:

bent thus, the same amount of ink flows more gradually

Intro:2 Writing position and ink reservoirs (see *The Calligrapher's Handbook* for information on nib sharpening)

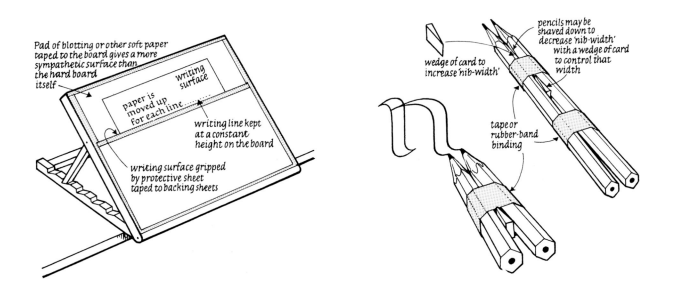

Pad of blotting or other soft paper taped to the board gives a more sympathetic surface than the hard board itself

writing surface

paper is moved up for each line

writing line kept at a constant height on the board

writing surface gripped by protective sheet taped to backing sheets

pencils may be shaved down to decrease 'nib-width' with a wedge of card to control that width

wedge of card to increase 'nib-width'

tape or rubber-band binding

Intro:3 Adjustment of writing surface on the board

Intro:4 Double pencils

INTRODUCTION

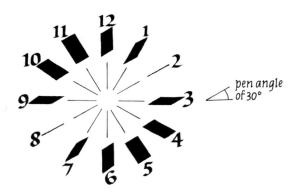

Intro:5 Edward Johnston's 'clock' diagram

Edward Johnston devised a 'clock' diagram to illustrate how to understand and remember the way in which strokes written in different directions with a constant pen angle achieve different results (**Intro: 5**). For instance, the pen's edge kept at a constant 30° (the 2 to 8 line of the clock) gives a variety of weights as it travels from 12 to 6, 1 to 7, 9 to 3, 10 to 4 (the movement being in the direction easiest for the pen without pushing against its edge; top to bottom, left to right, rather then the opposites). These variations explain why in some alphabets the recommended pen angle needs to be varied occasionally to achieve similar weights of some 'thicks' and 'thins': for example, if it is desired to keep a fairly consistent weight for both the vertical thin of a roman capital **N** and the diagonal thin of the **A**.

Until particular letterforms become familiar it is probably best to use a smooth-surfaced paper for practice, to minimise problems of the friction between the pen and the paper surface. Also for ease of working, a non-waterproof 'Indian' ink (sometimes labelled as being of ground 'Chinese') or 'sumi' ink, flows from a metal pen more easily than waterproof Indian ink which contains shellac as a waterproofing agent. Shellac can cause the ink to clog the pen as it evaporates during writing. Once the particular alphabet being practised is familiar, it is easier to concentrate on the effects created by different papers, by the use of ground stick ink which allows greater control over the ink's consistency, or by watercolour or gouache if colour seems desirable (most coloured inks are rather 'thin' in both the senses of consistency and saturation of colour). For ease of practice, a fibre-tip broad pen will suffice and will avoid those problems of friction between pen and paper mentioned above. Make sure, though, that it is satisfactorily sharp for sufficient distinction between thick and thin strokes, otherwise the essential nature of broad-pen strokes may be disguised (these pens can be sharpened to a certain extent with a scalpel but eventually they become too much softened to be useful). A 'bleedproof' pad of paper may be necessary to prevent the dye in these pens from staining through the surface of the sheet.

Paper for more finished exercises is likely to be of the hand- or mould-made variety, commonly described by the stock-ist as suitable for drawing, watercolour painting or print-making. It will be found in three main surfaces: 'rough', 'NOT' and 'hot-pressed'. The last two are more likely to be sympathetic surfaces for calligraphy unless a large size of pen (maybe one with a rather blunt edge) is used and a rough outline to the letterform is suitable for the purpose in mind. This sort of effect can be quite dramatic but edges away from the formal scripts that are the concern here. *The Calligrapher's Handbook* gives more extensive advice on inks and writing surfaces.

Edward Johnston proposed a set of 'Rules for copying a manuscript' which it may be useful to re-state here, although it is more productive to think of 'studying' than of 'copying'. These are: **1** pen angle (of edge to horizontal), **2** height (number of nib-widths) to weight, **3** shape (e.g. of **o**: is it circular, oval, flat-sided, pointed, etc?) **4** number of strokes (to make each letter), **5** order (of these strokes), **6** direction (of these strokes: starting/finishing point; up, down, left to right), **7** the same speed (at which the original might have been written). To those may be added the relationship of height/depth of ascenders/descenders and capitals to the x-height, which strongly affects the overall texture of an area of writing. It may also be noted that the first rule refers to the generally applicable angle but this may vary for individual letters/parts of letters, or for main parts of letters compared with terminals of strokes or serifs.

The 'modernised' exemplar illustrated alongside a historical precedent will by its nature be something to be copied as a starting point. In a lecture or workshop situation the presentation of an alphabet can be made more effectively. It can be written freely and any necessary minor corrections rewritten. This is an excellent method of teaching because of the immediacy of the visual experience, the possibility of direct comparisons and the fruitful opportunity for easy question and answer. If exemplars are presented in a freely written way in print, that freedom will, by its nature, produce inconsistencies and inaccuracies which need to be explained and corrected by copious notes to the student. The alternative is to present what one hopes is as 'model' an exemplar as possible, consistent in all its details. This almost inevitably means that it will have a stiffness about it which is certainly not a criterion of good calligraphy but which is a simpler and clearer point of departure. It is the method adopted here.

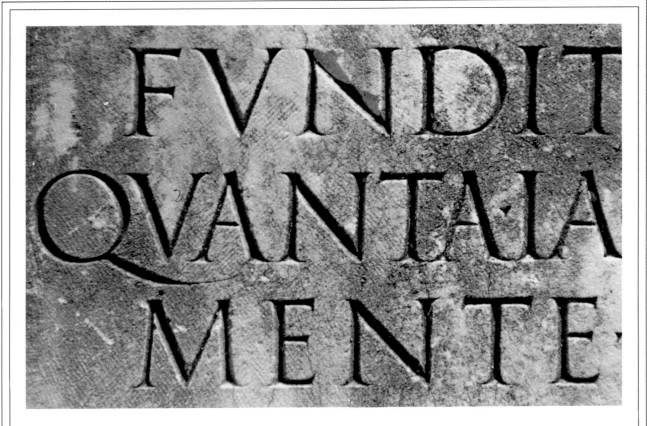

Roman Capitals

Rome, still in situ by the Via Appia, inscription of the 1st or 2nd century AD. Overall size (excluding moulding) about 6′ × 9′ (c 183 × 274cm). The individual letters are 3 inches (7.5cm) high.

It was the Romans who, between the late 1st century BC and the early 2nd century AD, perfected formal monumental lettering. Their subtle use of shading and entasis on the stems of the letters, the graceful serifs, the carefully balanced proportions and the generous, even spacing – all combine to form beautiful, harmonious and extremely legible inscriptions. 2000 years later, the classical Roman alphabet remains the criterion for evaluating lettering quality.

Despite the ravages of time, the inscription illustrated here retains something of its original grandeur. It was an enormous undertaking (it probably contained all of 500 letters), yet it is superbly consistent and very carefully planned. Without resort to abbreviations or word-splitting at the end of lines (which appear in most other classical Roman inscriptions), each of the lines has been accurately centred – hence the very close spacing of line **2** and the openness of line **3**.

The letters are more deeply cut and of heavier weight than those of the better-known Trajan Column inscription and the **A**, **M** and **N** have serifed tops. Nevertheless, as in the Trajan, carefully balanced proportions are given to each group of letters. In this inscription the **O** is circular:

D, **G** and **N** are not quite as wide as their height; **M** is just wider than its own height. **A**, **V** and **T** assume medium width; **P**, **R** and **X** are narrow; **E** and **S** are very narrow (only half as wide as their height); and so on.

These subtle variations in proportion enhance the individuality of the appearance of each letter and so aid legibility.

CHAPTER 1

SKELETON ROMAN CAPITALS

This alphabet is based on formal inscriptions of Classical Roman times which show evidence of a common tradition of geometrical relationships between the letterforms. We have no documentation of this but existing inscriptions seem to make it self-evident. This relationship is easy to see in the proportions of simpler forms of letters. In the most complex letters it is more difficult to trace and most easily remembered, perhaps, as a system of related widths (**1:1**).

It is tempting to believe that the mathematical and engineering skills of the Romans found some expression in the execution of their letterforms which had achieved an extremely high standard of design and craftsmanship by the first century AD. Only capitals were used, although there is maybe the first inkling of an emergent minuscule in the very freely written informal versions used for documents.

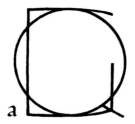 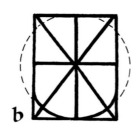  

 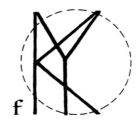

1:1

a Round – based on the circle: **O Q C G D**
D falls short of the full width of the circle by enclosing a shape equal in area to the circle. C and G, by an imaginary extension on the open side, do likewise. Ends of curves of C and G flatten considerably compared with the circle. Upright of G about half its height.

b Rectangular/diagonal: **H U N T Z**
Based on a rectangle of equal area to the circle. Base of Z is a little wider than its top for reasons of balance.

c Half-width, round or rectangular: **B P R S E F L**
S is obviously based on two small circles within the common height, therefore half the width of the large circle. Ends flatten in the same way as C. P and R tend to have their centre division a little below centre to emphasise their typical forms, the leg of R extending beyond the top bowl for reasons of balance.

d Triangular: **A V X**
At this point the simple notion of areas related to the circle ceases to be useful. By trial and error it will be found that the same width as group **b** gives a counter compatible in area to the other letters.

e Multiple shapes: **M W**
M is not the same as W upside down. If the centre of M is made the same as V, the near-upright outer strokes bring the whole width to that of the circle, or a fraction wider. Note that this makes the two angles between outer and centre strokes smaller than that of the centre V, whereas the W has three equal angles, as though it is two narrower Vs placed together.

f Intermediate widths: **K Y**
A width between group **b** and **c** seems to be right. Try making them the width of group **a** or **c** and it will be seen that they look too wide or narrow. As the centre point of K needs to be slightly above mathematical centre, its lower leg extends slightly beyond the top. The centre of Y can be very slightly below mathematical centre to emphasise its typical form.

g Thin: **I J**
They are obviously only the width of their strokes. The tail of J is to distinguish it from the related I sound. It can be on or below the baseline, but it is sensible to relate it to the circular forms of other letters – a quarter of the group **c** letters' circle, perhaps.

A B C D E F G H I J K L M N O P Q R S T U V W X Y Z & R U & Q

1:2 Alphabet of skeleton Roman capitals with alternatives for some letters

In Renaissance times artists interested in letterforms sought to reproduce the system of proportions by geometric calculation and the use of ruler and compass. Trying to draw the subtleties of the Roman alphabet by these means was doomed to failure, but this period is specially significant in that its revival of the Classical Roman forms coincided with the invention in the West of printing from movable metal type. The forms that were preserved by this medium included the Roman capitals which were enjoying a contemporary revival. They became an enduring part of our tradition of letter design and remain familiar through everyday reading matter. Some early typefaces were revived at the beginning of this century, after a period of degeneration in the latter part of the preceding one, and, more recently, have been adapted for use in digitised computer typesetting. They have, therefore, become a basic and abiding part of our heritage of letterforms and are a good starting point for study. Our minuscule letters, both 'roman' and, later, italic also owe their parentage to these capitals.

The proportions are illustrated in **1:1** in terms of simple geometrical relationships. Renaissance theories about these were convoluted but it is wise to keep the system as simple as possible. Where it may be tempting to relate the compound letterforms such as **M** to geometry, it is wiser to use a simple aide-mémoire of groups of similar widths which can be simply referred to during periods of drawing or writing. When skeleton forms are used later as a basis for heavier weights of letter and the complications of varying weights created in different parts of the letter by the broad pen, the proportions may need to be subtly and systematically altered. However, the underlying structure will still need to relate to the same system of proportions.

Even these simple forms in a thin monoline need some subtle variations from the simple geometric figures which are their basis. For instance, the apparent size of a circle which just touches top and bottom 'writing lines' will appear smaller than rectangular forms that have more contact with these lines, so the circle needs to extend slightly above and below the lines, as do other curved letters. The visual centre of a rectangle is slightly above its mathematical one, so letters which are divided across the middle, such as **B** and **E** need their centre points slightly above mathematical centre (an exception is **A** which, being a triangle, needs its crossbar to be slightly *below* the mathematical centre between the top and bottom lines so as to divide its counter in a visually balanced way). If the lengths of the horizontals of **E** are made exactly the same, the centre one will appear to protrude, and the top one will seem slightly longer than the base by optical illusion, so to compensate visually the bottom stroke is made slightly longer, than the top, the middle one shortest of the three.

The skeleton capital alphabet is worth practising in three basic ways. Firstly with a monoline pen, fibre-tip pen or pencil which gives the required weight of line at one stroke (the weight should not be greater than about one twentieth of the height of the letter).

Secondly, with a small size of broad pen (pen angle 30°), its width about one twentieth of the letter height (so that it remains a 'skeleton' rather than approaching the thin and thick weighted qualities of the broad-pen Roman forms).

Although the edge of such a pen should encounter little surface resistance, it would be best to practise the pen lifts and order of strokes discussed on pages 19–20.

13

Thirdly, with a monoline pen, fibre-tip pen or pencil a little thinner than the required stroke of the letter. This is more of a drawing action where the required shapes are built up from a sequence of strokes. It makes one aware of the subtle way in which slightly varying weights of outline define the counters (any significant difference of weight should follow the distribution of thick and thin which the previous exercise produced), and of slightly varying thicknesses at junctions of letter strokes. The illustrations were drawn in this way.

Although this book is essentially about broad-pen forms, the monoline exercises with this and the succeeding alphabet will be helpful in their concentration on basic forms without concern over the way in which the broad pen produces thick and thin strokes.

Once this alphabet is learned, variations in curved forms may be worked out which do not have the circle as a basis. Proportions of other letters will be altered in sympathy (**1:3**). However, if the new basis is radically different, say an oval **O** of half the width of the circle, it will be seen by

1:3 Varying proportions of skeleton Roman capitals

experiment that other proportions will have to change by less than this divisor - an **E** of this alphabet would look very skimpy if less than half its **O**. So, in the system of Roman proportions, the narrower the alphabet, the more similar the widths of wider and narrower letters will be.

14

CHAPTER 2

SKELETON ROMAN MINUSCULES
AND NUMERALS

The minuscule alphabet developed from the capitals by various routes. Uncial letters show several characters at an intermediate stage in this process. It took about seven centuries to develop what we would recognise as the minuscule alphabet we are familiar with in everyday reading. In a manner parallel to that of the capitals, it was a Renaissance revival of an earlier hand, the Carolingian, which made sure that it endured as a typeface.

Often the capital and minuscule alphabets will be used together, so it is obvious that their proportions and some details of construction need to have much in common. The circular **o** is common to both, so the proportions of this alphabet may be based on it also. The greatly different letterforms here mean that there are smaller differences in width than in the capitals but more letters which share part of the circular form in greater or lesser degree (for instance, those with archforms top or bottom). These last two factors are important in that they help the calligrapher to write rhythmically – there is a natural rhythm inherent in the skeleton proportions.

It would be a conveniently neat theory if ascenders were the capital height, and the x-height half that. That would allow a word to have sufficient 'typical outline', on which its legibility relies in the quick reading commonly associated with passages of minuscules. But in practice we come up against one of those important visual factors which make it important to modify the neat theories. That is, in passages of text with letters following the proportions outlined above, it is found that the capitals appear larger in scale than the minuscules, and the ascenders and descenders appear unnecessarily long to define adequately the word outline. So normally those proportions need to be modified as in **2:1**, or as seen in the typeface used in this book.

As with the capitals preceding, this alphabet is basic to others, so it is worth learning thoroughly and practising in the same ways including the order of strokes discussed on pages 19–20, (obviously if used together the two alphabets would be made with the same tool).

2:1 Relationship of ascenders and descenders to capitals. Ascenders and descenders are about two-thirds or three-quarters of x-height. The top of capitals should be slightly below that of ascenders.

2:2 Alphabet of skeleton Roman minuscules

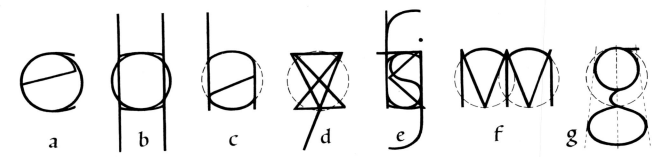

2:3

a Round – based on the circle: **o c e**

   The top of **e**, sometimes with a horizontal cross-bar, is less in area than its base.

b d b p q

   Compare with capital **D**.

c The width of a rectangle equal in area to the circle, but with a part circle within their form: **a h u**

d Triangular: **v x y z**

   Equal in width to group **c**. Relationship of top and bottom of **x** and **z** as for capitals (**1:2**)

e f t k s r i j l

   A little narrower than group **c** (except for **i l** which are obviously the width of their stroke). Curves of **f j t** related to the circle, but not as full an arc as the archforms of **h** and **n**.   **s** looks too narrow if made as a smaller version of the cap **S** so it is made to extend beyond two mini-circles. **l** with a rounded tail might

sometimes be seen included in this group. This stems from using the *Ramsey Psalter* (page 24) as a model, as Edward Johnston advocated, and the tail is a remnant of the horizontal of capital **L** becoming a minuscule. It seems, however a slight anachronism when related to the generality of letterforms in current use.

f Compound: **m w**

   Double width of **n** and **v**.

g **g** arrived at its 'normal' roman form (as distinct from the alternative round **g**) by a rather complex development from the capital **G**. For reasons of visual balance it is not sufficient to draw two small circles, with a joining stroke, between the top of x-height and descender line. The base needs to be wider, so it has become an oval, with the centre joining stroke requiring the top to be less than an **o**. It may be thought of as being contained within a truncated cone.

Numerals are based on similar skeleton forms of letter with an oval (to distinguish zero from **O**) as basis; apart from **1**, they are of similar width.

In typographic terms, numerals are of 'ranging' or 'non-ranging' varieties. 'Ranging' applies to numerals that are all of the same height as the capitals they accompany. 'Non-ranging' numerals have 'ascenders and descenders', which match the texture of minuscules. Either form can be chosen,

therefore, to suit the appropriate context. Through the conventions of typographic usage it is usual to see non-ranging 1, 2 and 0 equal to the x-height (and sometimes 4), the remainder having ascenders and descenders alternating between odd and even numbers. The length of ascenders and descenders is usually slightly less than that in minuscules for reasons of visual balance.

ABC 1234567890

Axbp 1234567890

2:4 Ranging and non-ranging skeleton numerals and their relationship to cap height and x-height

The Little Bird

A NURSERY RHYME

Once I saw a little bird
come hop, hop, hop
And I cried, 'Little bird will
you stop, stop, stop?'
I was going to the window
to say, 'How do you do?'
But he shook his little tail

and away he flew…

HOW VAINLY

MEN THEMSELVES AMAZE

To win the palm, the oak, or bays,
And their incessant labours see
Crowned from some single herb or tree,
Whose short and narrow-verged shade
Does prudently their toils upraid;
While all the flowers and trees do close
To weave the garments of repose!

Fair Quiet, have I found thee here
And Innocence, thy sister dear?
Mistaken long, I sought you then
In busy companies of men:
Your sacred plants, if here below,
Only among the plants will grow:
Society is all but rude
To this delicious
> SOLITUDE.

Hazel Beney
The Little Bird. The text based on English Carolingian
minuscules. Note how the cut stencil shapes harmonise
with the formal letterforms. Gouache, screen print and
gold on Fabriano Artistico paper. 13″ × 7$\frac{1}{16}$″
(33 × 18 cm) 1990

Joan Pilsbury
The Garden by Andrew Marvell. Versal heading and
initial, a fine italic and capitals written with a rather flat
pen angle. Quill writing on vellum with black stick ink,
watercolour and raised gold. 12$\frac{3}{4}$″ × 11$\frac{7}{16}$″ (32.5 × 29 cm)
recto of double-page spread. 1987
(Crafts Council collection)

Square Capitals

London, British Library, Royal Ms. 14.C.iii, folio 2ʀ.
(Jerome's Latin version of Eusebius' *History of the World*).
Written in northern Italy, late in the 15th century, by
Bartolomeo San Vito. This detail is shown at 2½ times
actual size.

Written Square capitals are closely related, in their
letterforms and spacing, to inscriptional Roman capitals.
As the individual letters are complicated to make and take
up a great deal of space, they were only rarely used
historically for writing the whole text of a book. (Just two
such ancient manuscripts are known, the *Codex Sangallensis*
and the *Codex Augusteus*, both from the 5th century.)

Humanist scribes, however, revived the use of Square
capitals, giving them pride of place as titles, colophons
and line initials. The Paduan scribe, Bartolomeo San Vito,
made a speciality of them – his distinctive capitals are
elegant, expertly written and beautifully spaced.

These capitals are alternately coloured and gilded in
the manner typical of this scribe: line 1 is gold and green;
line 2 purple and gold; line 3 gold and blue; and line 4 red
and gold. They are directly written with great freedom

and confidence. The pen angle is much flattened,
generally about 15° (apart from diagonals, which are
nearer 40°), but there is a liberal use of manipulation (pen
twisting and angle changes) and of additional strokes in
the formation of certain serifs (see **I** line 2), stem endings
(**T** line 1), curves (**S** line 2) and flourishes. Note San Vito's
own characteristic **R** and his tendency to give a slightly
backward lean to **A**, **V** and, occcasionally, **M**.

CHAPTER 3

SLANTED-PEN CAPITALS (SQUARE CAPITALS)

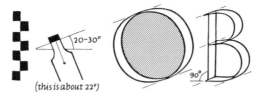

(this is about 22°)

This is an alphabet formed by the broad pen's giving natural weighting to the skeleton capitals, with the pen generally held at a constant angle (but see below for exceptions).

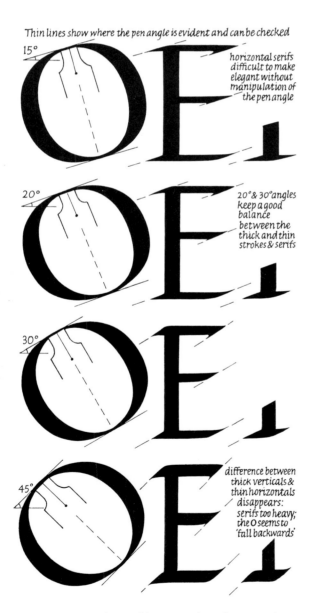

Thin lines show where the pen angle is evident and can be checked

15°

horizontal serifs difficult to make elegant without manipulation of the pen angle

20°

20° & 30° angles keep a good balance between the thick and thin strokes & serifs

30°

45°

difference between thick verticals & thin horizontals disappears: serifs too heavy; the O seems to 'fall backwards'

3:1 A comparison of typical letters made with pen angles of 15°, 20°, 30° and 45°

The 20° or 30° pen angle gives a satisfactory but different stress to the curves and different weight to serifs. In the **E** it preserves a satisfactory contrast of thick to thin stroke — the thick giving the main strength to the upright, the thin being the minor horizontal or serif. If the pen angle is increased beyond this, the contrast becomes unhappily less distinct. For instance, if the angle is 45°, what are normally thick verticals and thin horizontals become much the same weight, which disrupts the thick/thin pattern normally set up by the broad pen throughout the alphabet. The increased angle of stress in the round letters also makes them appear uncomfortably to 'fall backwards'.

If the 'clock' diagram and the diagrams of skeleton capital proportions are compared, it will be seen that the pen moves in many different directions to form the main strokes of these letters. Studying merely the rightward-sloping diagonals of **A**, **M**, **Z**, we find four different angles varying from approximately 45° to 80° to the horizontal.

One of these, the diagonal of **Z**, is the main stroke of the letter, the others minor strokes. If we adopt the view that it is desirable to preserve some consistency of thick and thin throughout the alphabet, it follows that occasional manipulation of the 'constant' pen angle may be advisable. This is not as drastic as it sounds, for the difference between the thicks which the pen will make on strokes whose angles vary by as much as 20° or so is not really enough to be worrying. Apart from the special case of **Z**, it is the difference between thins that is more noticeable and requires this sort of extra care. In the case of **Z**, keeping the regular pen angle produces three fairly thin strokes and this is not in keeping with the pattern of thin/thick elsewhere. The alternatives are to turn the pen to 45°–50° to produce thicker top and bottom strokes and thinner diagonal or, my preference, to turn the pen to almost 0° for the centre stroke, making this the major thickness. These changes of angle for the sake of refinement are marked on the illustrations with an asterisk.

Once the skeleton form and the weight and angle of the pen (which will give weight to the skeleton) have been decided, the next basic consideration is the number, order and direction of the strokes which will make the letters (ref. items 4, 5, 6, of the list on page 10). Most formal scripts will be written relatively slowly, or at least deliberately, and will involve a number of pen lifts and separate strokes to complete a letter. All the alphabets in this book presume, unless it is otherwise noted, that the direction of the pen will be from top to bottom and from left to right, with pen

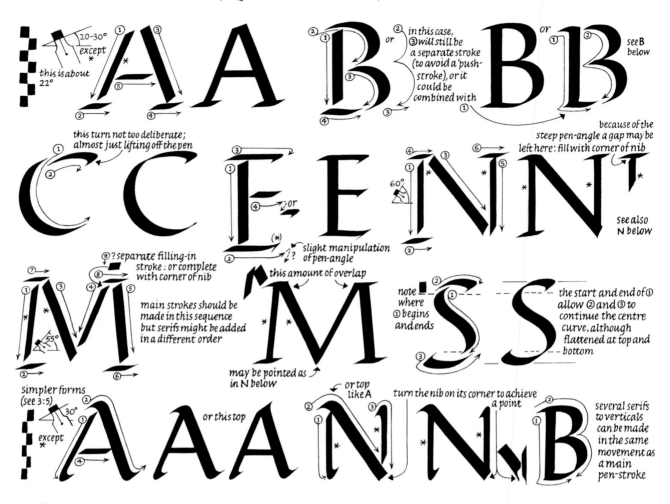

3:2 The pen strokes required for sample capitals

3:3 A formal alphabet with cross serifs (made with pen lifts)

lifts to avoid at any time pushing against the breadth of the pen. **3:2** illustrates this sufficiently for directional signs on every letter to be avoided. It will usually be obvious from the detail of illustrated alphabets whether a pen lift is involved or not. The first alphabet (**3:3**) is obviously rather more formal than the second. The first may be the best

to start on − the deliberate pen lifts to make serifs give a simple strength − for the apparently more simple forms of the second alphabet (**3:4**) can easily lead to the sloppy forms shown as ones to avoid (**3:5**). The curves of the terminals of these letters should not intrude on the essential structural form.

3:4 A more informal alphabet with simple terminals (no pen lifts for terminals)

proportion too wide: gives a 'collapsed' appearance

cross-bar too high: top part of counter looks too small

exaggeration of pen's natural emphasis on the down-stroke: letter seems to fall backwards

the opposite of the previous fault

cross-bar too high and letter too narrow

separation of the two diagonals tends to leave ugly counters: letter too wide

letter too wide: angles of counters should not be equal—M is not like an upside-down W

unequal outer counters give an unbalanced look

incorrect overlaps on top: LH counter therefore appears lower & smaller

centre stroke too straight: counters too unequal and different in form

ends of curves not flat enough, serif curves exaggerated: looks too similar to 8

centre junction too 'pinched', lower counter too small

main strokes should remain straight, serif curves a minor proportion, to achieve a 'strong-looking' letterform

etcetera, for all letters with straight strokes

3:5 Shapes to avoid

em facerdos fcin

adhuc defiderar

Quid uobis uide

runt eum efle reu

fpuere eum: et ue

Humanist Minuscules

West Berlin, Kupferstichkabinett, Ms. 78.D.17, folio 111R
(A *Missale Romanum* written by Arrighi in Rome, 1520). It
is signed and dated by the scribe: 'Ludovicus Vincentinus
Scribebat Romae An. Sal. MDXX'. This detail, of a Gospel
reading from St Mark 14, is shown at 3 times actual size.

Arrighi was a professional scribe employed by the
Papal Chancery and a Writing Master who published the
first illustrated instruction book on the Chancery Cursive
style of Italic: *La Operina* (see page 34). Of all the
manuscripts known to be produced by Arrighi, however,
only two are written in minuscule – this one and another
discovered by Vera Law in 1977 (now in a private
collection in London).

In Italy the use of Carolingian minuscule (see page 26)
was not superseded by angular Gothic scripts (as in other
European countries), and there are many examples of fine,
round Italian minuscules dating from the 12th century.
Early in the 15th century Italian Humanists in Florence
revived the Carolingian script for the purpose of copying
out classical texts. This hand was later refined by the
Writing Masters and adopted by the first Italian printers.

This mature script combines soundness of letter
structure with good spacing and rhythmic flow. The **o**
and related letters are round (though perhaps a *little*
narrower than the two overlapping circles of the *Ramsey
Psalter*, page 24), and the 'minim' arches (**h,m,n** and **u**) are
broad. Note the very flat pen angle, and the various types
of serifs used on the ascenders. The script perhaps betrays
the influence of typographic letters in the formation of the
serifs, especially in the use of manipulation and the corner
of the pen in completing the short **s** (which incidentally is
only used at the end of words). Square capitals are
employed here very satisfactorily as initials.

fquam gallus cantet bis

CHAPTER 4

SLANTED-PEN MINUSCULES

Three varieties of this type of letter follow, based in their detail on the historical model preceding each one. They are presented in reverse chronology so that the first two match the order of the slanted-pen capitals and the suggested order of study. Humanist minuscules relate to the first alphabet of capitals which was based on a model from the same period, and 'Foundational' minuscules match in detail the capitals with simple terminals. Carolingian minuscules, although they were the progenitor of the others, appear to have an antique quality compared with, say, the typeface of this book.

Humanist

These letters follow the skeleton minuscules on page 15 and, in the same way as the slanted-pen capitals, demonstrate the form achieved by the broad pen's weighting. As in the capitals, the pen angle is 20°–30°; similar pen lifts and direction of strokes are employed. A further visual continuity is the use of similar serifs. As before, changes of pen angle are signalled by an asterisk. The reason for the changes is the same – the preservation of a reasonable consistency of thick and thin throughout the writing.

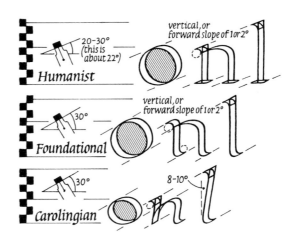

4:1   Three varieties of slanted-pen minuscule

4:2   Typical strokes and pen lifts for Humanist minuscules

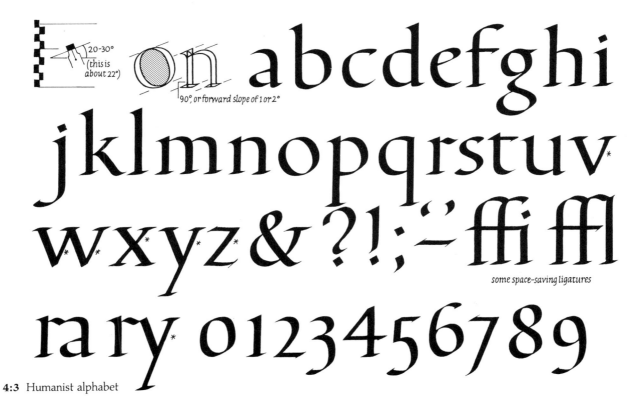

some space-saving ligatures

4:3   Humanist alphabet

23

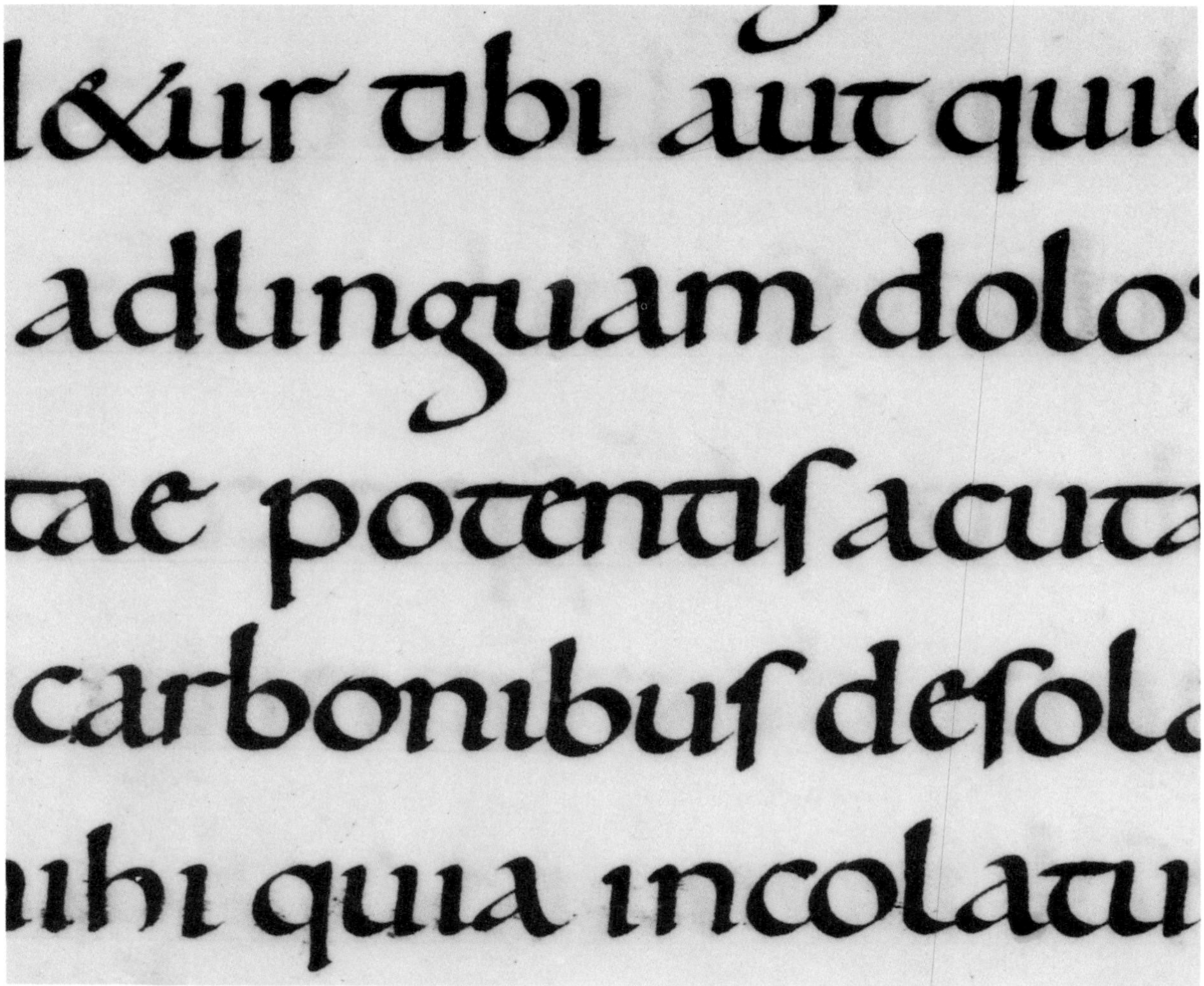

l &ur тbı aúr quıc

adlınguam dolo

тae potntaf acuta

carbonıbuf defola

ıhı quıa ıncolaтu

English Carolingian Minuscules

London, British Library, Harley Ms. 2904, folio 164R. (*The Ramsey Psalter.*) Written in southern England, possibly at the Cathedral Priory at Winchester or at Ramsey Abbey, *c*974–986. This detail is shown at twice actual size.

This script is the most distinctive and imposing English version of the French Carolingian minuscule. Written 150 years after the *Grandval Bible* (see page 26), it is one of the finest achievements of English penmanship. Edward Johnston, in his first book, recognised that 'this extremely legible MS would form an almost perfect model for a modern formal hand' (*Writing and Illuminating, and Lettering*, 1906), and he later used it as the basis for his 'Foundational Hand'. Johnston used the term 'foundational' not only because the hand makes an excellent starting point, but also because it is capable of much adaptation and development.

This powerful and assured hand is very soundly constructed and almost completely free of mannerisms. The **o** is round (the outline is like two overlapping circles), and many letters take their form from it: **b, c, d, e, g, p, q** and **t**. Even the arched letters **h, m, n** and **u** vigorously echo the curve of the **o**. The strength of the script is further enhanced by the weight of the letters (whose 'x-height' is often less than four pen widths) and the insistent pen angle of 30° to the base line, but the slight forward stance allows some life and movement to the hand. Note the usually 'clubbed' serifs (made by a second, overlapping pen stroke), the rather uncertain form of **a**, the weak tail of **g** and the use of long **s**.

maui &exaudiu

a symmetrical archform, starting at the base of the serif curve, beginning the thickening of the stroke from that point

b cross-serifs made with a separate pen stroke, extending equally each side of the main uprights. The slight curve at each end of the cross-stroke is a result of putting down and picking up the pen rather than making a deliberate curved stroke

c flattened curve avoids a heavy junction (compare base of p)

d serif only on one side of upright

e symmetrical archform (reverse of n above)

f x-height g pen-lift here if desired

h symmetrical arch, wider & flatter than others

i visual centre of balance of the whole shape

4:4 Details of construction for the writing of Humanist minuscules

varying pen-angles

lower part projects too far

curve not part-circle

looks like a numeral 8

uprights not straight

archform starts too low (is not a part-circle)

terminals are different shapes: LH lower one almost closes counter

too much 'pull' on lower curve tips the letter backwards

too much curve on a cross-serif

opposite of the previous letter

centre stroke should be a continuous double curve

terminals exaggerated, especially the lower one

too much turn-down of curve on top gives a heavy junction

weak junction of archform & base of upright

lower terminal too large

4:5 Shapes to avoid

'Foundational'

Edward Johnston's name of 'Foundational' is used though some letters and details have been adapted for the sake of consistency. But the alphabet is essentially similar in that it is based on the same historical model. Antiquated forms such as the round **t**, sloping **a**, and long **s** of the historical model have been avoided. This alphabet has the same skeletons as the Humanist but uses a slightly heavier pen weight, a slightly greater pen angle and simple terminals (Johnston used beaked serifs at the top of ascenders and on uprights of **i** and **j**). These qualities ally it to the second of the preceding capital alphabets. Although it is basically very similar to the Humanist minuscule, it is interesting to note what a difference the details make. It is included as a separate alphabet rather than merely a variety because students may already have been introduced to it as the basis of their studies on account of Johnston's continuing influence on the teaching of calligraphy.

As before, changes of pen angle are noted by an asterisk. The need for these changes is greater because of the heavier pen width-to-height ratio in this alphabet. The changes of angle will naturally be rather studied and slowly made until the mental picture of the alphabet becomes remembered. Then the slight manipulations become second nature and will be written at greater speed.

The turn-over of terminals is rather less than the width of the nib from the top and bottom line; the sideways extension no more.

The basic upright may be thought of as having three parts: a straight centre part and two curved terminals – but written in one fluent stroke. Avoid losing the uprightness of the centre and overstating the curves for this results in a weak form.

Archforms create a rhythm of the same shape in the letters **a, b, d, h, m, n, u**, as well as referring to the curved forms.

upright, or sloping forward by 1 or 2°

alternative letters

this g & y derived from italic

alternative beaked serifs

4:6 'Foundational' alphabet with constructional notes

Carolingian Minuscules

London, British Library, Add. Ms. 10546, folio 411v. (*The Moutier-Grandval Bible*.) This single-volume Bible was written at the Abbey of St Martin, Tours, France, *c* 835. This detail is shown at 4 times actual size.

The emergence of the Carolingian minuscule is one of the most important developments in the history of calligraphy. The hand of Charlemagne's Court Scriptorium in the last decade of the 8th century provided the immediate model for the beautifully legible book script used at St Martin's. This minuscule is a mature script of enduring quality. It was to be copied and adapted in succeeding centuries by scribes in England, Germany and Italy. Humanist scribes revived it, early in the 15th century, as a most suitable hand for the copying of classical texts (see page 22). The first Italian printers then adopted it, and it has remained the basis of Western typography to this day.

The script of the *Grandval Bible*, though very small, is extremely consistent and well formed. Even some of the larger scripts of the Gospels and Psalters made at Tours (e.g. British Library Harley Mss. 2790 and 2793) lack the rhythm and structure of the example shown here.

The cursive ('running') character of the script is encouraged by the size and speed at which it was written, and can be discerned in its slight forward slope, the wideness of such letters as **a**, **d**, **m**, **n**, **q** and **u**, and the 'branching' construction of **m**, **n** and **r** – usually written without pen lifts. The angle of the pen is generally flat, between 25° and 30° to the base line. Note the forms of **a**, **f**, **g**, long **s** and **t** – so typical of the mature Carolingian minuscule, the very tall ascenders with their heavily 'clubbed' serifs (possibly made by first pushing the pen upwards and then moving over and down to make the vertical strokes) and the wide interlinear space.

Carolingian

This alphabet appears to have a less formal texture because of its slope and the cursive branching forms written without pen lifts. In larger sizes, these letters may require rather slower formation than that of the historical examples, even to the stage of being made (in the case of the **n**) in three strokes rather than one (**4:7**). This may also depend on the nature of the paper surface to be used. The basic skeleton can be seen to be the precursor of the slanted-pen minuscule forms already illustrated, but it is based on a noticeably wider **o**. This may be because of the heavier nib width-to-height ratio. Greater pen weight necessitates more care in forming the counters of the letters and one way to do this is to widen the skeletons. The speed of writing of the historical model, which can be deduced from its rhythm, coupled with the pattern of its branching forms will be seen to be a precursor of Italic, (page 31). For the sake of illustration, the alphabet is shown a good deal larger than the historical model's actual size, and practice on such a scale will probably be helpful. There are, however, difficulties with this size of pen in the making of the branching strokes where there is a need to push against the edge of the pen. The 'club' terminals of the original may also have been made in one movement, upwards, then turning over and downwards, partly cover-

4:7 Pen lifts for larger sizes of **n** and other archforms

ing the first stroke. To make it slightly less archaic-looking, beaked serifs, similar to other slanted-pen ascenders, have been suggested.

Carolingian did not have a directly-related capital alphabet to accompany it. It was usually paired with Uncials and/or Versals, the former more usually used within the text. The use of such capitals tends to reinforce the 'period' appearance. That may be acceptable, depending on the context, but, if not, a modified form of simply-written roman capitals, as illustrated, can be used. Capitals can be made to agree with the minuscules by having the same slant and by the introduction of details such as the branching from the first stroke of appropriate capital forms such as **B** and **D**. An occasional more Uncial form may also be introduced without becoming too 'period'.

Because of the relationship of the basic angle of the pen to the slope of the letters, the changes of pen angle previously necessary to create a consistent pattern of thicks and thins are no longer required in this alphabet (except for **Z**).

the varied line-spacing is merely to accomodate the unusally long ascenders and descenders in the minimum area

m,n,r,u,z,2,3,7 are made in one stroke (but see 4:7). On a small enough scale, so could c,e,g,q,v,w, with only a small push-stroke. Except for the small filling-in stroke of the beaked serif, so could b,d,h,l, also be a single stroke.

4:8 'Carolingian' alphabet with constructional notes

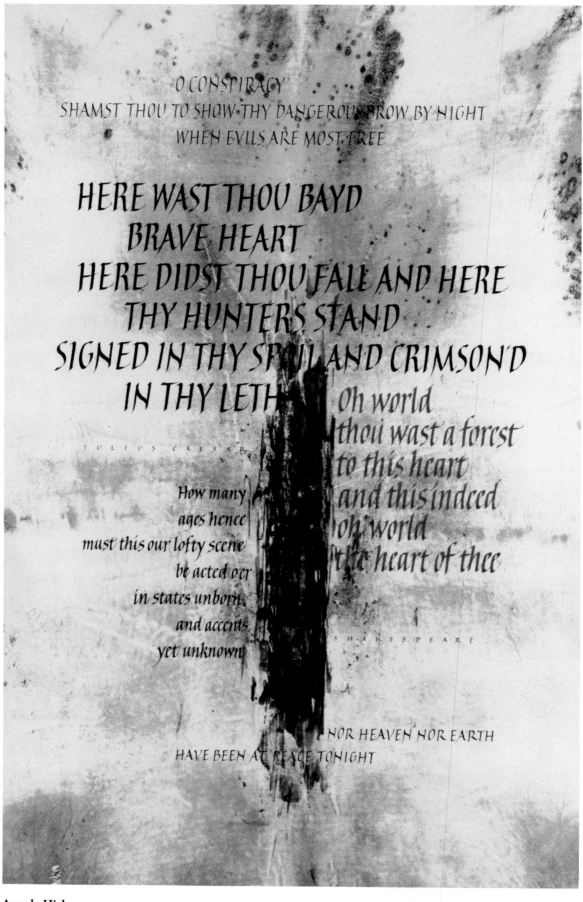

Angela Hickey
'Here wast thou bayd...' from *Julius Caesar* by William Shakespeare. Italic capitals and minuscules in greys and dark red gouache on vellum with heavy hair marks. $25\frac{1}{8}'' \times 16\frac{15}{16}''$ (64 × 43 cm) 1990

CHAPTER 5

ITALIC MINUSCULES

The distinctive forms of Italic can be related historically to the same sources as roman minuscules and were developed largely through a need for greater speed of writing. The Carolingian minuscule, with its cursive, branching tendencies, was revived in Renaissance times and is probably the letterform that developed into the distinctive Italic hand. Formal variants were developed for different purposes – the three forms given here will provide the calligrapher with a wide range of possibilities. Italic is perhaps the most used letterform of recent years and can range comfortably from the very formal to the extremely informal once the basic character is understood.

The early Italic scripts made use of accompanying upright roman capitals. The subsequently-developed Italic capital may be thought of simply as a roman capital with the slight forward slope and compression of proportions to agree with the oval **o** which is the basis of the minuscule.

As well as the slope, oval **o**, and the cursive branching archforms, Italic has a few distinctive letterforms which developed from the mode of writing. The closed **a**, **f** often with a flourished tail, **g** with a simple looped tail, **k** with a closed bowl and sometimes a round form of **y**, combine with the other characteristics to give a distinctive texture to writing in this hand. Its full development at the time of the first typefaces led to its place as one of the major letterforms of our tradition. The normal type 'family' of roman capitals, roman lower case and italic, with bold varieties of one or more, allows for all normally required degrees of emphasis in most of the everyday printed matter we read.

In terms of calligraphy we can proceed to identify three main forms of Italic: Cursive Italic, with an elliptical **o**; 'Sloped Roman' (a comparatively recent, but conveniently descriptive, typographical term) with a slightly flattened oval **o** and, more importantly, the roman archform; and Pointed Italic, with a pointed **o** and archforms. The last originates from a mixture of sources: not only did some sixteenth-century scribes write a slightly pointed oval but the wood-engraved version produced to print 'copy books' exaggerated this tendency because an engraving tool makes a pointed shape more easily than a true oval in small sizes. Later, Gothic 'Bastarda' hands also developed a pointed cursive form and Edward Johnston wrote a hand which had generally pointed characteristics.

Italics usually have a slope of about 5°, but not necessarily. The relative narrowness and archforms are sufficient to distinguish the hand from roman even if it is upright. A more formal Italic, written slowly, with pen lifts to make archforms, may be expected to have beaked serifs to suit its character, and may include the roman version of **g**; a less

formal one may have simple hooked terminals. But there are no strict rules about this any more than for most other factors of letter design, once the traditional forms are understood and the new context respected.

The passages of text on the endpapers show the textures produced by the three styles discussed. Note that the degree of compression and slope has been kept much the same so that it is obvious how the basis of each different **o**, with archforms to suit, affects the texture. The occasional ligature joining letters of the cursive indicate its semi-formal nature and the relative speed of writing it. By contrast, the Sloped Roman appears the most formal and can be seen to be more slowly written.

5:1 Three varieties of Italic

Maria mater Dei pietate
plenissima, summi regis fi
ia, mater gloriosissima, m
er orphanorum, consola
io desolatorum, via erran

Cancellaresca Formata

London, Victoria and Albert Museum, 86.C.107. *Arte de Escrevir* by Francisco Lucas, page 27. (Wood-engraved instruction book of various writing styles.) The first edition of the Lucas Manual was published in Toledo in 1571 and the second, from which this reproduction is taken, was published in 1577 in Madrid. This illustration is shown 1.7 times actual size.

During the Renaissance period a number of wood-engraved Manuals were produced which showed various styles of writing and lettering. Despite the incredible skill of the engravers the printed exemplars are inevitably removed from the feel of the original writing, especially as most of them have the background of the block cut away to simulate the appearance of black writing on white paper. Lucas has successfully minimised this discrepancy by writing large and by having the *letters* cut out of the wood.

Two distinct forms of Italic script were taught by the Humanist Writing Masters: a narrow, rather pointed version with tall hooked ascenders, 'Cancellaresca Corsiva' (Chancery Script, see page 34), and a slightly wider version with more rounded arches and shorter serifed ascenders, 'Cancellaresca Formata'. Although Lucas calls his example 'Bastarda' it is a fine example of the 'Formata' style – despite the use of hooked ascenders.

Note the flattened oval shape to the **o**, the 'one-sided' curve to the arches of **m**, **n** and **h** (matching those of **a** and **u**), the branching on **m** and **n**, etc. occurs halfway up the first vertical stroke (or even a little higher). A pen angle of 40° to 45° is used to maintain fine strokes on the branches. Capitals, unless flourished, are not as tall as the ascenders.

Bastarda grande llan

Cursive Italic

The essence of the cursive archform is that it originally developed from considerations of speed and economy – made in one stroke of the pen at the same time as the uprights. It involves a push stroke with the broad edge of the pen – something that has previously been advised against because it produces tension between nib and writing surface and because it can inhibit fluency. The slope of the letter, combined with the fairly steep pen angle, and the usually lighter weight of the letter compared with roman, all mitigate this difficulty. If a heavier letter is required, especially if it is to be written on a slightly abrasive paper surface, it may be necessary to form the letters with pen lifts between separate strokes (**5:2**). Usually a sympathy between writing surface and pen (and its sharpness) is required to write a truly cursive italic. Even when a slowly-written, formal version is being written it will be found that a good lower archform is more easily achieved at some speed, whereas arches at the tops of letters can be written slowly without the form deteriorating.

5:2   a   b   c

a The usual Cursive Italic construction in one pen stroke
b Larger sizes and heavier weights may more conveniently be constructed with more than one stroke.

c Comparison of Cursive Italic and 'sloped roman' archforms

5:3 Cursive Italic alphabets and numerals

Sloped Humanist Minuscules

London, Victoria and Albert Museum, Ms. L.1349–1957 (KRP.A.22), folios 12v (above) and 17ʀ. (Jacobus Ragona *De Artificiali memoria*.) This manuscript, made *c* 1465 for a member of the Ragona family, was once thought to be the work of Antonio Tophio but is now attributed (by Dr Albinia de la Mare) to the Paduan scribe, Bartolomeo San Vito. This detail is shown at 5 times actual size.

This is quite a small book (the page size is $6\frac{1}{2} \times 4\frac{1}{8}''$ (16.5×10.5 cm) without illumination. The dedication/title page and the beginning of the text pages are set out in coloured Square capitals, in the scribe's usual manner (see page 18). The rest is written in elegant minuscules with paragraph initials in blue and the opening words in pink.

The unusual hand by the very experienced scribe, San Vito, seems to be halfway between an upright Humanist minuscule (see page 22) and a 'Formata' Italic (page 30). It could perhaps best be described as a Sloped Roman. The arch strokes of **m** and **n**, etc. are made separately (whereas 'Corsiva' and 'Formata' apparently intend continuous minim strokes without pen lifts), and they have a more rounded shape. Some letters are very narrow (particularly **o**, **c** and **e**), others are generally so – **h**, **m** and **n**, but **d** and **q** (and occasionally **u**) are wide. Perhaps the formal character of the script could be improved by maintaining a more consistent width. Note the usual 30° pen angle, the idiosyncratic 'flying' serifs on the ascenders, and the occasionally shared stems on curved letters.

Sloped Roman Minuscules

This retains the slope and compression of the Cursive Italic but has roman archforms, i.e. they spring from the tops of uprights, as in roman minuscules (see page 23), rather than from further down the uprights as in the Cursive Italic (**5:3**).

Although the shape will vary according to the nib width-to-x-height ratio chosen, a circular roman **o** compressed to the width of other italic **o**s will tend to look 'flattened' rather than elliptical or pointed. The historical example shows this well. The same thing happens with the roman archform, a part of the curve of a flattened circle, which will be seen in **b**, **c**, **d**, **e**, **h**, **m**, **n**, **p**, etc.

Whereas in the other forms of Italic a rather steep pen angle, together with the slope of the letters, makes it easier to write an upright plus an archform in one continuous stroke, even though the pen has to be pushed for part of the stroke, in the case of Sloped Roman, a flatter pen angle is needed if an archform and its connection to the upright are to be properly formed.

oh abcdefghijkl
mnopqrstuvwxy
alternatives with simple terminals
z&fgynpru ABC
DEFGHIJKLMN
OPQRSTUVW
XYZ&0123456789

5:4 'Sloped Roman alphabets and numerals'. Capitals are the same as for the Cursive Italic alphabet but with flatter curves consistent with the flatter oval base-form.

idicio cadere uisum e

i Iuriſconſultiſſimum

n uero eloquentiſſimu

i, quantum fieri poti

ſſimis characteribus

Cancellaresca Corsiva

London, British Library, Royal Ms. 12.C.viii, folio 2v.
(*Apologues of Pandolfo Collenuccio*.) Written in Rome *c* 1517,
undoubtedly by Arrighi (Ludovico Vincentino). This
detail is shown at 4 times actual size.

This manuscript is a luxury volume with highly ornate
illuminations, and the page shown is part of the Address
to Henry VIII of England to whom this book was
presented.

Arrighi, a professional scribe employed by the Papal
Chancery, was the first Writing Master to produce by
wood engraving an illustrated Instruction Book for
writing 'Cancellaresca Corsiva': *La Operina*, published in
1522 and reprinted in 1533. This Chancery Cursive was a
rapid style of Italic writing developed in the Papal
Chancery for briefs and other less formal documents.

The style used for this manuscript is extremely
compressed and its sharp, angular quality is emphasised
by the steep pen angle (45°–55°). Although there are very
few ligatures and joins, and the writing is quite widely
spaced, the impression is of rapid, informal handwriting.
Note the almost pointed character of **a**, **o** and **n**, the low
branching on **m**, **n**, etc., sometimes a little below the
halfway point of the first vertical stroke, and the hooked
ascenders. Note also the overheavy horizontal strokes on
f and **t** (due to the very steep pen angle), and the rather
weak 'Uncial' form of **h**. As is usual at this time, long **s** is
used within words and short **s** at the end of words (or in
a **ss** ligature).

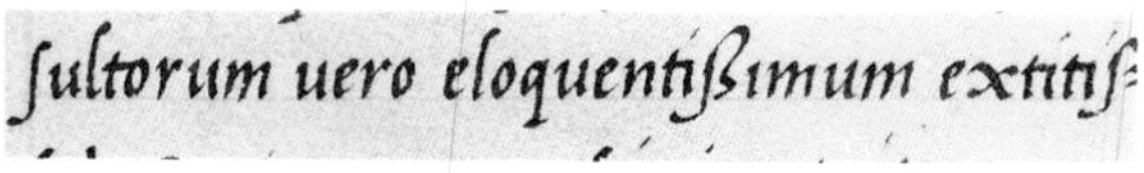

ſultorum uero eloquentiſſimum extitiſ

Pointed Italic

Pointed Italic has the same sort of slope as the Cursive Italic but with a different basic **o**, and with archforms to suit. Some capitals can adopt a form similar in character to the minuscules' pointed arches. **B**, **D**, **F**, **P** and **R** allow a branching shape which follows that pattern and may be derived from Gothic Cursive (see page 55). The alternative round form of **E** allows a certain pointedness, also reminiscent of Gothic, but narrower in proportion to suit the compression of Italic. Alternatively, if a Gothic character is

to be avoided, an emphasis on the flat tops of **B**, **D**, **P** and **R** can be used to create a contrast to the pointed arches in the same way as do the tops of **a**, **d**, **g**, etc. Early examples of Italic often used upright Roman Square Capitals as initials in a manner that contrasted the proportions of their circular **O** with the Italic **o** of elliptical or more pointed form.

Some of the wood-engraved examples of the sixteenth century are worth examining as examples of a pointed letter, although the pointedness may be due to a certain extent to the use of an engraver's tool, as previously explained.

5:5 Pointed Italic alphabets and numerals

THE AIR SHINES WITH A MILD MAGNIFICENCE ...LEAVES, ...VOICES, ...GLITTERINGS...
AND THERE IS ALSO WATER WINDING IN EASY WAYS AMONG MUCH GREEN EXPANSE
OR LYING FLAT IN SMALL FLOODS, ON THE GRASS AS THE WHOLE SOFT SONG OF THIS TREMULOUS INSTANT
WATER WHICH IN ITS WIDESPREAD CRYSTAL HOLDS ITS ROOTS, THE WALLS' BLAND GREY OF REBIRTH AND PEACE
TREMULOUS - YET BENEATH HOW DEEP AIR'S GEMS, THE WALLS' BLAND GREY
TIMELESSNESS OF AN AFTERNOON! AIR'S GEMS, THESE BELONG TO NO DATE
SLIM SPIRES, HOPE-COLOURED FIELDS: THESE BELONG TO NO DATE

OXFORD: A SPRING DAY
·DAVID GASCOYNE·
SCRIBE·STAN KNIGHT

MILD MAGN
NATER V
DING IN EASY V
...THE WHOL
...ITS ROOT

Stan Knight
Oxford: a Spring Day by
David Gascoyne. Freely
written, simplified
Versals in multiple
shades of grey and pink
gouache on Arches
Aquarelle hot-pressed
paper. 16½″ square
(42 cm) 1989

Left: detail

Sally Teague

Aries. A wide variety of Italic minuscules, capitals and
flourishes. The variety of writing texture is held together
by the comparatively simple structure of vertical columns
of text. Written in red, white, grey and violet gouache on
black paper. $21\frac{1}{4}'' \times 32\frac{1}{2}$ (54 × 82.5 cm) inside mount. 1990

Early Uncials

St Gallen, Stiftsbibliothek, Ms. Cod. 1394 (pages 51–88). (*Codex Sangallensis*, Gospel fragments.) Only 20 folios of this manuscript survive, 16 of them collected between pages 51 and 88 of this codex. (Ms. 1394 also contains the remaining folios of the famous ancient Square capital manuscript (see *Historical Scripts* B2). It was written in Italy in the 5th century. This detail is shown at $2\frac{1}{2}$ times actual size.

Most of the earliest surviving Uncial manuscripts have their origins in northern Africa – the oldest datable Uncial is from Hippo and was written between 396 and 426. Later, Uncials were used in Italy (particularly in Rome), often for Biblical texts, and thus through missionary activity the script spread to other parts of the Empire, including Britain. However, the notion that Uncials were deliberately devised (during the reign of the Emperor Constantine, 306–377) as a Christian book hand cannot be maintained. Ancient scripts (and inscriptions) with clear Uncial characteristics which long pre-date Constantine (e.g. the *De Bellis Macedonicis* fragment *c* 100 and the Timgad Inscription of 2nd or 3rd century), the existence of *some* Christian texts written in Rustic capitals (e.g. the fragment of St John's Gospel in Aberdeen and that of the

Epistle to the Ephesians in Florence), and of at least one pagan author, a Cicero, in Uncials in the 4th century (Vat. Lat. 5757) – all cast grave doubt on this common assertion.

This Italian script is a fine example of the slanted (or 'natural') pen Uncials. It is unusually sharp and precisely made. The angle of the pen is generally kept at 30° though one or two letters seem to be written with a slightly flatter pen, e.g. the cross stroke of all **E**s and the curve of **E** (line 4). A steeper angle is used for the arches of **H** (line 5) and **M** (line 3) – in fact the **M** on line 3 seems to suggest that the hairline of the arches was made separately from the final main curve. There could perhaps be more consistency of shape – **E** ranges from flat to square, **N** (line 2) is rather wide and **T** too narrow. Nevertheless this is a marvellously rhythmic and soundly constructed script, and rivals even that of the better known *St Cuthbert (Stonyhurst) Gospel*.

CHAPTER 6

UNCIALS

Uncial forms were largely complete by the fourth century AD. They have their origin in Roman pen capitals, but the pen gradually modified certain characters such as the **E** into a form which could be written with greater economy of strokes. For similar reasons letters such as **D** and **H** not only changed their form but produced a latent form of ascender. Much of the alphabet shows, in fact, signs of a developing minuscule.

Two varieties are illustrated – one written with a slanted pen and one with a flat pen.

The slanted-pen form is to be recommended for initial practice, being simpler to write. The flat-pen form looks grander and more formal and may be used for an occasion where those qualities are desirable.

The essential roundness of Uncials is a form natural to the broad pen; it can make a fine page of writing but its 'antique' character needs to be employed with discretion. It

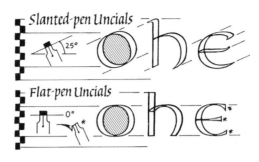

6:1 Two varieties of Uncial

makes a useful foil to other textures of writing where a contrast is desirable, or (as in Carolingian manuscripts) it can be useful as a heading or title to text of a contrasting letterform.

Slanted-pen Uncials

Although these Uncials have virtually the same skeleton forms as those of the next alphabet, the steeper pen angle means that this version can be written with more speed and it is appropriate then to give it simpler terminals. There seems to be no obvious constructional reason for

changes of pen angle for the arches of **H** and **M** in the historical example; they are probably characteristics of the work of one particular scribe working freely and at some speed. The extension of 'ascenders' and 'descenders' is very small, the better to emphasise the regular texture between the horizontal writing lines.

6:2 Uncial alphabet and numerals made with a slanted pen

Late Uncials

Durham, Cathedral Library, Ms. B.IV.6, folio 169*. (A fragment of the Book of Maccabees now pasted down as a flyleaf so that only one side is visible.) Written in Italy in the 6th century. This detail is shown at $2\frac{1}{2}$ times actual size.

The monastic communities at Wearmouth-Jarrow, founded by Benedict Biscop in 674 and 681 and later led by Ceolfrid, had a very active scriptorium. Both abbots had visited Rome and brought back works of art, manuscripts and relics for the monasteries. The Wearmouth-Jarrow scribes developed their own expert version of the Uncial script, using Roman manuscripts as their model. It is not certain that the example of the Uncial form shown here was copied by them (there are a number of structural differences between it and the English style), but the text certainly was. The famous *Codex Amiatinus*, written at Wearmouth-Jarrow, shares with this fragment the reading of 'marima(m)' instead of the more usual 'maritimam'. There are only two manuscripts known to take this reading: one an Italian manuscript surviving in Northumbria, the other a Northumbrian manuscript surviving in Italy!

The later form of Uncial, distinguished by its flattened pen angle, is often elaborately detailed, with much use of pen manipulation — especially for the serifs. It is sometimes referred to as 'artificial' Uncial in view of the complexity of its construction. However, this example is fairly straightforward with excellent structure and nicely judged weighting.

For most curving strokes the pen angle is about 10° from the baseline, but even flatter for the main stroke of **A** and the letters with vertical strokes (note the twist of the pen at the bottom of **F**, **I**, **P** and **R**), and about 40° for the bowl of **A**, the long arm of **D**, and the first vertical and the diagonal of **N**. Note the hairline details of **G**, **N** and **X**. Pen twisting is needed for the formation of the serifs. In this hand the most difficult ones have been simplified: the lower serif on **C**, **E** and **S**, the tail of the **G** and **X**, the first vertical of **N**, and the left hand serif on **T** (cf. other 'artificial' Uncials in *Historical Scripts*, B6 and B7). In this script the interlinear space is approximately the same as the height of the letters.

Flat-pen Uncials

These are more difficult to write: the pen angle is uncomfortable to maintain unless the pen is cut (if a quill or reed), or ground (if a steel nib) to a 'right-oblique' edge (see **9:2**). It can be seen in parts of the exemplar how the straight-cut steel nib has tended to stray to a more comfortable angle (the base of uprights of **H**, **K**, **R**). The formation of formal serifs on curved letters and horizontal strokes requires tricky manipulation of the pen. If a quill is being used, it may be found a little easier if the split is made off centre.

The flat pen angle inevitably leads to a more slowly-written letter. The basic **O** is slightly wider and the serifs more deliberate and formal, most particularly at the ends of curved letters and straight horizontals. These require pen manipulation. Note that the historical exemplar economises on the number of serifs, mainly at the base of letters. The writing is on a small scale and, perhaps because of this, the top serifs have become exaggerated, which leaves little scope for them to be repeated at the base. The weight of the historical example is slightly heavier than that of the previous alphabet and this characteristic has been followed, though it is not strictly necessary (see Chapter 18).

6:3 Uncial alphabet and numerals made with a flat pen. Constructional notes include a drawing of an unequally-split quill and its use in the formation of serifs.

41

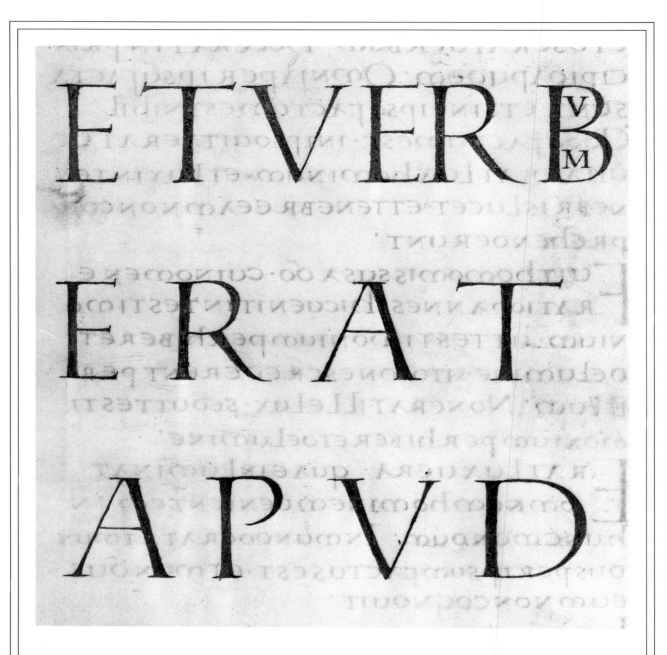

Compound Roman Capitals

Paris, Bibliothèque Nationale, Ms. Lat. 9388, folio 151r. (The Metz Gospels.) The manuscript was written at Metz in northern France c 850. This detail, of the opening words of St John's Gospel, is shown at actual size.

Like other Carolingian manuscripts the Metz Gospels use, for 'display' purposes, elegantly written capitals based on the carved letterforms of classical Rome. The similarities of proportion, spacing and character are so marked that one cannot help feeling that these are pen adaptations, copied from actual inscriptions which were common throughout the ancient Roman Empire. Nicolete Gray refers to a manuscript of c 836, now in Berne, which has an alphabet seemingly copied from an inscription.

These gilded capitals, three writing lines high, were first outlined with separate strokes of a narrow pen and then the body of the main stems was filled in. The inner ellipses of the rounded forms have a distinct backward tilt, and the vertical strokes have 'entasis' (i.e. a slight swelling towards the top and bottom) — features reminiscent of classical inscriptional letters. The serifs, however, have been adapted to calligraphic form and are sometimes simple hairlines rather than 'bracketed'.

CHAPTER 7

COMPOUND ROMAN CAPITALS

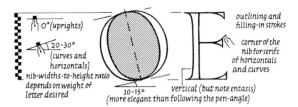

Once again the skeleton proportions of Roman capitals apply to this alphabet. The study of slanted-pen capitals will also be helpful in giving a clear idea of the disposition of shading, and of thick and thin strokes. The pen is used in a manner essentially different from the simple slanted-pen action – more a deliberate drawing – and this produces a difference of detail which is close to that of lapidary inscriptions (page 11). The subtle refinement of entasis and bracketing of serifs is similar to that produced by the chisel. This way of using the pen is almost the same as for Versals (page 47). In fact, if the weights were similar it would only be a matter of serif formation, angle of stress and occasional variation of pen angle that would distinguish the two. The method, as well as the detail which springs from it, produces a more formal, rather grander letter than simple pen capitals. It tends, therefore, to be more appropriate for producing larger letters for titles or headings, as the historical example well shows.

The nib width-to-height ratio indicated in the introductory diagram is a suggestion only. Because of the method of compound construction, this ratio is very variable. The exemplar was written with a fairly rigid steel pen; a more flexible pen used with more pen manipulation would give slightly different detail. My preference is simply to hold the pen at 20°–30° for round letters and horizontals, then vertically for uprights and diagonals, with some manipulation for serifs or for curves and horizontals. There are obviously other ways of achieving a similar result. Probably the simpler the better at the start.

  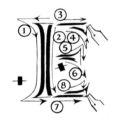

a third, filling-in stroke (possibly more),° is made between the main outlining strokes

turning the nib on its corner for serifs needs the ink to flow well so that most of the filling-in is achieved at the same time as the outlining

° e.g. at the swelling of serifs

7:1 Constructional notes

ABCDEFGH IJKLMNQPR STUVWXYZ

7:2 Alphabet of compound Roman capitals

COMPOUND ROMAN MINUSCULES

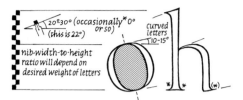

Whereas simple-written forms show the full effect of the broad pen's use, these minuscules allow conscious drawing of the details of shading and serifs. The pen is here being used as a drawing tool comparable with the chisel or burin of other media. If a simple system of pen angles is retained, the action of the pen is still apparent in the distribution of weighting and in the constructional strength. For formal letters such as these, it is important to retain the strength of obviously pen-made forms and not to allow a desire for innovation to spoil this strength. It is therefore advisable to become proficient in simple pen forms before attempting these more complex ones.

Minuscules may be made in the same way as capitals, with a double stroke of the pen, following the skeleton form and the distribution of thick and thin of slanted-pen minuscules. They are, perhaps, of most use for such occasions as titles where a large size offers opportunity for subtleties of drawing best achieved by this method;

the complexities are probably not worth trying on small sizes where a simple pen construction will be adequate. These letters were made with two simple overlapping strokes (without a third infilling). The control over regular thickness of stroke is by the amount of overlap, whereas in the construction of the capitals control is provided by the amount of white space left between preliminary outlining strokes. Of course, if capitals and minuscules are to be used together, the same construction is preferable in order to achieve a balance of weights. A slight exaggeration of shading compared with the simple pen form is natural to the method and gives a distinct detail to the letters. It is not advisable to over-exaggerate; the amount of overlap of the two strokes will be the guide. A similar form can be written with a flexible pen with some degree of pressure exerted. This is probably best attempted only when the student has experience of a range of letters and has developed facility with the broad pen.

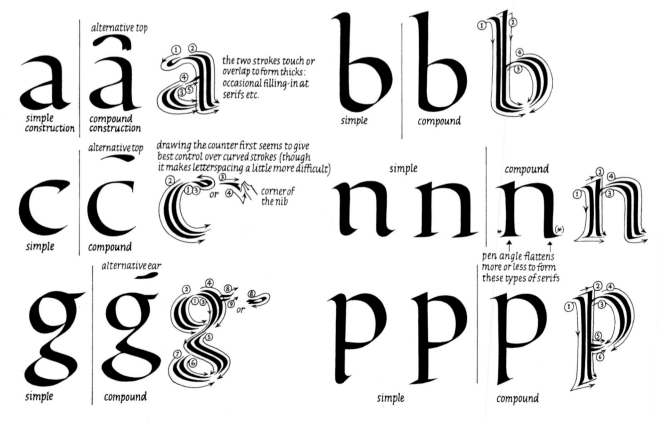

8:1 Comparison between simple and compound Roman minuscules

o *corner of nib*

abcdefghi

jklmnopq

rstuvwxy

alternative terminals

z&acrs

8:2 Compound minuscule alphabet

Versal Capitals

Winchester, Cathedral Library. *The Winchester Bible*, folio 109R. This huge, four-volume Bible, with a page size *c* 23″ × 16″ (586 × 407 mm), was written soon after 1160. Bishop Henry de Blois encouraged the production of manuscripts at the Cathedral Priory, and this must have been his greatest undertaking. Capitals heading the First Book of Kings are shown at actual size.

A number of lavish Bibles were produced in England during the 12th century including the Bury Bible (now in Cambridge), the Hugh de Puiset Bible at Durham and the Lambeth Bible. In these Bibles Versal capitals were used for the opening words of the individual books. Often they were fitted round imposing historiated initials and, in consequence, were distorted or contracted. On this page, however, the scribe has had adequate room for the long colophon so we can appreciate the undistorted letterforms and open spacing.

The robust capitals are written in alternate lines of red and blue, in the manner typical of the period. Their weight matches the heavy texture of the writing (arranged in tight columns) and the richness of the illumination on the page. The vigorous outlines of the letters were drawn (two writing lines high) with a fine pen (whose size can be determined by the vertical stems of **N** and **M**). The main strokes were 'flooded' in, while the outlines were still wet, to ensure a flat even layer of rich colour. Note the 'Uncial' form of some of these letters and the whimsical variations of the capital **A**. The **N** is perhaps structurally unbalanced and too narrow, and the 'Uncial' form of **H** has rather a weak arch stroke.

CHAPTER 9

VERSAL CAPITALS

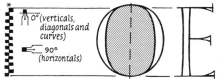

The name originates from the medieval tradition of using compound letters as initials to verses. Such letters were also used as initials to chapters or to give emphasis to a heading or title. This remains a typical use.

They are written/drawn in much the same way as compound roman capitals, with one difference. That is, the angle of the pen remains vertical or horizontal for all letters unless it is manipulated for serifs. Although Versals may be thought of as having the same skeleton forms as compound roman capitals (only needing to be varied if the weight of thick strokes becomes very heavy), this difference of pen angle results in significant difference of detail. Because of the pen angle, there is naturally a vertical stress to round forms, rather than the angle of the roman capitals, and a considerable difference between the thin strokes of round letters and those of the horizontal straights of letters such as **A** and **E**.

The introductory diagram is a suggestion of nib-width-to-height ratio. The pen width should be chosen so that the thicks are produced largely by the two outlining strokes, with a third one infilling. More work needed on infilling reduces the immediate freshness produced by the essentially simple basis of construction. This vigour and directness of drawing is a notable feature of the better historical examples. Especially if colour is being used, or gesso for gilding, a more flexible pen, with a longer than normal slit, allows the infilling to be done with a generous amount of writing medium flowing from the pen. This implies cutting a quill to suit these conditions, although a metal pen is adequate for most circumstances. It is helpful if the nib is cut, or ground if a metal one, to an oblique edge to facilitate the vertical pen angle (**9:2**).

It is less uncomfortable to turn a pen with this type of nib to the horizontal position than it is to turn one holding a square-cut nib to the vertical position.

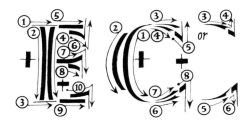

9:1 Construction of Versals

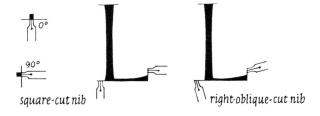

9:2 The use of square-cut and 'right-oblique' nibs

'normal' Versal construction, without hair-line serifs

movement given to the line by the angles of curves, serifs, uprights and 'horizontals'

a lighter weight: less shading produced by second outlining stroke of the pen (no filling-in stroke required): angle of pen for thin horizontals and verticals balances light weight of other strokes

in light weights of letters care is needed to avoid over-emphasis of the thickening towards terminals

thinner weight; diagonal emphasis as above; more gradual shading of curves

9:3 A variety of pen angles

VERSAL CAPITALS

The method of construction can be applied to more modern-looking forms which fall somewhere between the categories of Versals and Compound Roman Capitals, possibly something of a sans-serif variety with the pen angle changed to give greater weight to the thins of curved letters (**9:3**). The essential outlining method of construction also gives opportunities for simple forms of decorative capitals, for use as initials or possibly short titles (page 59).

9:4 A Versal alphabet and numerals with alternative archaic forms for some letters

CHAPTER 10

GOTHIC ALPHABETS

The name Gothic is rather imprecise but so are alternatives. Sometimes referred to as 'blackletter' – in the nineteenth century 'Old English' – the scripts in question are those which developed from the Carolingian hand, through the Middle Ages, with a gradual compression, angularity and increase in apparent weight. The term covers such varieties as Textura (or Quadrata), Prescissus (blunt endings to the base of some upright strokes), Fraktur, Schwabacher, Rotunda (the southern variety of Gothic which retained a roundness in its forms, as did the architecture of Italy and Spain) and Gothic Cursive (Bastarda). Three varieties are illustrated here to show the range of form and texture, some of the more confusingly illegible forms being avoided.

The first typefaces of the fifteenth century adopted the Textura form, and we might easily have been using these letters today as our normal reading, as happened in Germany until comparatively recent times. However, the interest in 'Classical' texts and the revival of the Carolingian hand in which available manuscripts were written, gained more favour and resulted in the tradition of most West European countries being based on the Roman. There are, therefore, associations attached to Gothic scripts which have to be taken into account in the context where they can be used, not the least of which is the sentimental connection in Victorian times with things medieval or 'Christmassy'. In a purely visual sense, the richness and weight can be effective, used in small amounts, as contrast to text in Roman letterforms. Used in larger amounts, their comparative lack of legibility needs to be taken into consideration.

Textura (or Quadrata)

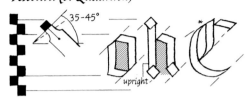

Rotunda

Cursive (or Bastarda)

10:1 Three varieties of Gothic letterform

John Woodcock
Heading from a certificate in the same series as the one reproduced opposite the title page.

THE MUSEUMS
FOUNDED 1889 · INCORPORATED 1930
ASSOCIATION
Diploma

Gothic Quadrata

Cambridge, Fitzwilliam Museum, Ms. 298, folio 90v. (*The Metz Pontifical.*) The manuscript was written and illuminated in northern France *c* 1300. This detail is shown at $1\frac{1}{2}$ times actual size.

This is a luxury manuscript probably intended for ceremonial use. Many of the pages have half their space devoted to elaborately painted miniatures, with much use of raised and burnished gold. The text has very few abbreviations.

Gothic hands of various sorts were in use from the 12th century onwards. The majority were characterised by lateral compression, heavy weight and severe angularity. 'Prescissus' scripts were those with abrupt lower stem endings on such letters as **m** and **n** ('prescissus' means 'cut off'). 'Textura' (meaning 'woven') scripts were rigidly written, closely packed and had lozenge-shaped terminations which enhanced the textural quality but made it difficult to read. 'Fraktur' scripts were a later development which introduced more cursive and deliberately stylistic forms. ('Fraktur' refers to the 'broken' character of some of the letters.) 'Rotunda', as its name implies, maintained a strong roundness in its construction (see page 52).

Many Gothic hands were mechanically rigid and lacked life. The large and expert 'Quadrata' script of the *Metz Pontifical* ('Quadrata' meaning 'square-shaped') retains the compression, weight and angular appearance of other gothic scripts but it has a true liveliness and rhythmic flow.

This script is sharp, unusually so for medieval manuscripts. Note the different construction given to **o** and **n** (and related letters). The **o**, with pen held at about 55°, begins with a shallow top stroke; the **n**, with pen nearer to 40° or 35°, begins with a longer hairline and a steeper top stroke. 45° is the usual pen position for the upstroke endings of certain letters (**a**, **c**, **e**, etc.). Note also the flatter pen angle needed to complete the ascenders and descenders. Occasionally two adjoining letters have shared stems.

Textura (or Quadrata)

The counter of the basic **o** is a parallelogram. This and a similar width to most letters except the compound **m** and **w** appear to make Textura a comparatively easy script to learn, despite the unfamiliar letterforms.

It may be tempting to produce all the angles of the skeleton **o** at the same 45° angle as the pen angle. To do so, however, will make the resultant texture of the writing boringly regular, though perhaps sufficient as a first-stage guide.

The historical model is written with a rhythmical fluency which gives life to the geometry underlying its shape. This may have something to do with the speed at which it was written but we would do well to look at the varieties of pen angle employed for it, consciously or not. The main differences to bear in mind are the relatively flat tops to 'archforms' compared with the steeper angles for serifs, especially those at the feet.

Capitals have historically tended to become rather decorative, with a wide variety of detail (page 58), but the exemplar shows a relatively simple alphabet, with a few alternatives added to indicate the sort of variety possible. Note the introduction of certain rounded letters, reminiscent of Uncials in form. These soften the angular quality of passages of text that consist of minuscules only. The habit of using a vertical within simple round capitals has the effect of avoiding the 'holes' in the overall texture formed by simple, open counters and of introducing a relationship with the verticality of the minuscules.

10:2 A line of Textura text with the pen and stroke angles indicated

10:3 Textura alphabets and numerals

Gothic Rotunda

European Private Collection. *The Carvajal Missal*, folio 46R. A Mass book in Latin for the Feast of the Epiphany, written and illuminated for Cardinal Bernardino de Carvajal (whose arms are painted in this manuscript). The book was made in Rome, 1520–1521, possibly by Matteo da Milano. This detail is shown actual size.

In Spain and Italy, rigidly angular Gothic scripts were largely avoided. In their place evolved a hand which was truly Gothic but more rounded in character – hence the name 'Rotunda'. It carried the weight and texture of other Gothic hands but not their excessive compression and harsh angularity. It was widely used, ranging from tiny personal Books of Hours to enormous ceremonial liturgical manuscripts (which often contained musical notation).

The Carvajal Missal is an outstanding example of a large Rotunda script written in black between double line ruling in pale red. The hand is clear, precise and strongly structured. A fairly consistent pen angle of 30° is used throughout – apart from the additional stroke required to finish the flattened stem endings on **f**, **m**, **n**, long **s**, etc., and the rather whimsical tail of **g** (which letter might be improved structurally by straightening its back stroke).

Rotunda

Although it incorporates a degree of compression and an emphasis on the vertical compared with Carolingian, this hand still retains a width and degree of roundness which makes quite a different-looking page from Textura. The archforms may be thought of as almost Roman in form, with just a little hint of angularity where the turn into the upright falls. The round letters are of generous width, even wider than a circle sometimes, with just a hint of the angular in the turn from top and bottom to sides. The broken **s** and tail of **g**, and the capitals are the only places where the full Gothic character is obvious. The Prescissus form of endings is common (see the alternative letters). This necessitates manipulation of the corner of the nib at the bottom of the letter or sometimes at the top of certain letters, or a slight pen lift with a change of angle (**10:4**). Elsewhere, the pen angle can remain constant.

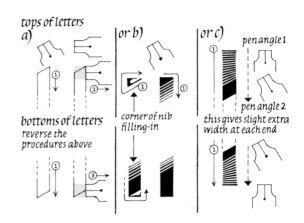

10:4 Prescissus endings to pen strokes

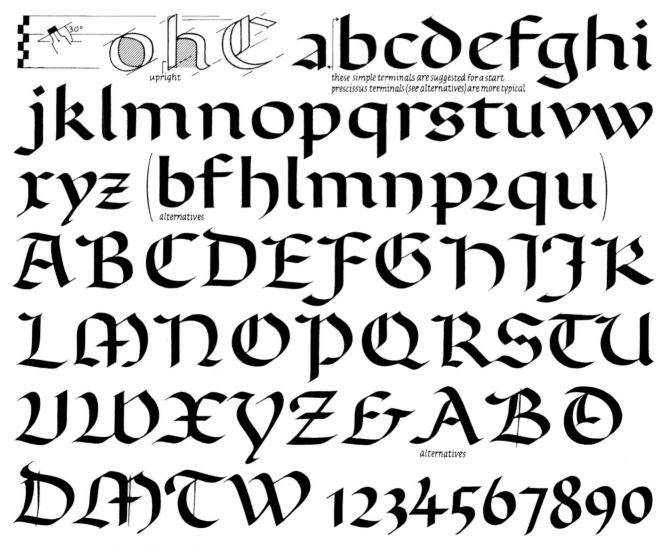

10:5 Rotunda alphabets and numerals

Gothic Bastarda

London, British Library, Royal Ms. 19.C.viii, folio 43v. (*Imaginacion de vraye noblesse.*) A book presented to Henry VII of England by Quintin Poulet, his librarian, in 1496. This detail is shown at 3 times actual size.

Alongside the formal Gothic hands there existed in the 14th and 15th century numerous cursive scripts used for legal, commercial and other documents. Bastarda is a bookhand which evolved, initially in northern France, as a formalised version of these Gothic cursives. Variations of the script appeared in England and elsewhere, and its popularity can be judged by the fact that it provided the basis for a number of early typefaces in France and England (e.g. for William Caxton's 1483 edition of *The Canterbury Tales*).

In Flanders, at the end of the 15th century, Bastarda was used, often at large scale, for luxury volumes written in French to meet the growing demand by wealthy and aristocratic bibliophiles. This manuscript is a typical example, lavishly illuminated and richly bound.

The script also appears stylish and confident — almost arrogant. It is slowly written and full of mannerisms and self-conscious vanities. Note the great flourish given to **f** and long **s**, and the tapering (nearly non-existent)

descenders. These, together with the idiosyncratic forms of **g** (an over-emphasised cross stroke), **m** and **n** (a mixture of arch shapes), **r** (seemingly a cross between **c** and **x** — see the beginning of line 2) and short **s** (an awkward, ugly construction — see the end of line 3) make Bastarda difficult to read fluently. Perhaps that was the point!

This hand is written with a very flexible pen (the heavy **f** and long **s** are a result of pen pressure) and its strong textural quality is enhanced by its forward slope. Its pen angle, about 30°, is flatter than that used for more formal Gothics. For the pointed curves, however, it is nearer to 40°. Some other letters (e.g. **x**, **y** — neither shown here — and the alternative **r** which is like the numeral 2) are written at approximately 45°. The branching strokes of **m**, **n**, **u**, etc. are steeper still, or perhaps made with the corner of the pen. Elaborate, matching capitals were devised for this form of script; a fine set was included in Tory's *Champ Fleury* published in 1529.

Cursive (or Bastarda)

This alphabet has elements reminiscent of both Carolingian and of Gothic Rotunda. The slope and branching archforms are a little like Carolingian but the archforms themselves, pointed and with sometimes a slight diagonal break in them, are more Gothic. The capitals, despite their slope and other small cursive characteristics, and the occasional hint of Uncials, are definitely Gothic in character.

The mixtures are various according to which historical model is being studied, something to be expected in a hand derived from such informal cursive origins.

The cursive nature of the script encourages ligatures between letters and they form a definite secondary texture. This effect, together with the weightiness of the letters, strongly emphasises the horizontal in a passage of text.

In the historical model, the exaggerated width of the upright pen strokes of **f** and long **s** and their markedly tapering tails are the product of a flexible pen used with variation of pressure and do not come easily from a metal pen used without pressure. A similar appearance may be retained if the pen is gradually turned on its corner towards the end of the upright stroke.

A typeface called Legend, designed by F. H. E. Schneidler in 1937, was modelled on such scripts but presented with more exaggeratedly flowing capitals. Some students may have been introduced to Bastarda by way of the typeface.

10:6 Bastarda alphabets and numerals

Rustic Capitals

Rome, Biblioteca Apostolica Vaticana (Vatican Library), Ms. Pal. Lat. 1631, folio 131r. (*Codex Palatinus*, works of the Latin author, Virgil). Written in Italy. This manuscript is usually assigned to the 4th or 5th century, but recent evidence suggests that it is more likely to be a 6th century copy of an earlier Rustic Virgil. This detail is shown at 2½ times actual size.

Rustic capitals were the very first Latin book hand. They are not a development from Square capitals, compressed to save space. The earliest examples of Rustics precede known examples of written Square capitals by more than 400 years. They were used until the Carolingian period as a book hand – the *Utrecht Psalter* is an outstanding example – and up to the onset of the Gothic period for 'display' purposes: headings, prefaces, colophons, etc.

The *Palatinus* has the appearance of an easy, natural hand, but this script is most difficult to write fluently and is not recommended for a beginner. Encouraged by the extremely steep pen angle, the letters are tall (approximately 7 pen widths), and very narrow (especially **E**, **L**, **P**, **R** and **T**). The angle of the pen in fact shifts a great

deal – 75° to 85° for vertical strokes, 60° for curved letters (including **S**), 45° to 50° for diagonals, approximately 45° for the base strokes of **E** and **L** (line 1, letter 6), and even nearly 30° for the short foot serifs (e.g. on **I**, **N**, **R**, and **T**). Note the extra tall **B** and **F** (to distinguish from **E**), and the occasional thickening of the base of vertical strokes. At the original size, it is not likely that this was produced by the twisting of the pen; it is much more probable that a second, quick stroke was overlaid. The texture of the writing in this manuscript is enhanced by the narrow interlinear space and the rhythmic letter spacing. No word spacing was employed at this time.

CHAPTER 11

RUSTIC CAPITALS

In its original form this alphabet was probably written quite quickly with pen or brush. The speed and relative informality may account for some of the detail which distinguishes Rustics from slanted-pen Roman capitals. For instance, in vertical strokes the pen sometimes changes angle from top to bottom, and slides into a base serif or other part of the letter in one continuing movement. It is easy to imagine how this arose from slight extra pressure and speedy writing with a flexible brush or reed — it does not come quite so naturally with a rigid steel pen and may be better executed in separate strokes.

At first sight, Rustics look as though they developed simply as an informal version of Roman capitals, but this does not seem to be the case. However, it may be useful to refer to the proportions of skeleton Roman capitals and earlier notes about changing the width of the basic **O**. With Rustics, the narrow letters such as **E** are of such minimum width that to reduce by a similar proportion a wide letter such as **M** would mean the almost complete obliteration of the counter by the overlapping pen strokes (unless the nib width were very fine, or the angle considerably varied). There is, therefore, a much greater difference between the proportions of the narrow and widest letters than in the case of slanted-pen Roman capitals. This, plus the changing pen angle, gives a quite different texture of writing. The particular rhythm of Rustics is emphasised along the top and bottom writing lines by the unusually heavy serifs caused by the pen angle.

11:1 An alternative pen hold for this alphabet

Because the pen angles are so different from those of alphabets so far discussed, Rustics need some careful study before anything like an appropriate speed can be successfully developed. It may also be found convenient to adopt a different hold on the pen (**11:1**) as an aid to preserving the unusual pen angles and, perhaps, for the right-handed to use a left-oblique pen. Altogether, a more varied use of the pen than we have so far considered. Different historical examples will no doubt suggest slightly different pen angles, proportions and details. In a hand with so much tendency towards the informal, the exemplar is a starting point only in the development of a hand with consistent formal elements that satisfy the individual (**11:2**).

11.2 Rustic alphabet and numerals with alternative versions of some letters

CHAPTER 12

DECORATIVE CAPITALS

This heading covers a vast range of letterforms and there are books which concern themselves solely with this subject. There is space here to consider merely some of the simpler forms consistent with the theme of this book, that is, those directly related to the construction of formal alphabets. This is taken as precluding letters decorated by painting or by drawing beyond the simple use of the broad pen. Drawing with a pen harmonises well with accompanying text.

Nevertheless, a single size of pen used at a variety of angles or more than one size of pen can produce a surprising range of decorative line or texture.

The most obvious decorated capitals, then, are those directly related to the preceding methods of constructing Compound Roman Capitals and Versals. The outlining procedure leads to some simple variants which can be effective for initials or short titles but which can cause difficulties when being adapted to the variety of forms of a complete alphabet. Begin with simple outlining which defines the white negative space. The proportion of this should stand in good contrast to the positive thickness of the strokes themselves. Variations can then be explored with, perhaps, a second weight of pen for visual interest. (Two weights of outline inevitably suggest a 'shadow' form and convention suggests that the heavier weight be on the right.)

The next stage is to try varying the shape of the main strokes themselves. This added complexity may best be confined to one main stroke of letters with a horizontally subdivided skeleton form, lest the decorativeness become too fussy. Then decoration within the counter can be tried. There are some very effective historical models where pen strokes made with simple changes of angle suggest stylised plant forms. The best of these are simply and vigorously drawn. The proportion of the skeleton form may need to be widened slightly to accommodate the flowing lines appropriate to this kind of decoration.

One list of possibilities reads as follows: **1** variation of the simple form of the letter; **2** variation of the compound construction; **3** decorative use of the counter; **4** use of space round the letter; **5** use of both **3** and **4**; **6** 'inline' decoration (i.e. within the thick strokes of the letter).

Within the limitations imposed by the broad pen, which can be used in different sizes, the possibilities listed above can be treated in a variety of ways: *a* abstract or semi-abstract forms or textures; *b* formal diaper patterns; *c* stylised natural forms or arabesques.

Colour(s) and/or metals may be added to the decoration or used without other decoration to give a simple contrast to the writing of the accompanying text.

12:1 Examples of decorative capitals freely drawn from historical models

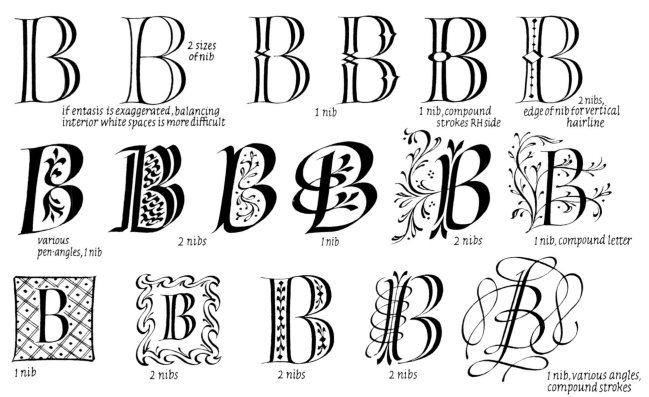

12:2 Individual letters covering the suggestions made above

ABCDEFGHIJ
KLMNOPQR
STUVWXYZ&

'Dont's'
Don't allow decoration to overwhelm the letterform to the point of illegibility; *don't* use superimposed forms contrary to the letterform's natural shape; *don't* allow decoration extending beyond an initial to detach it too far from the rest of the word; *don't* allow the scale or visual character of decoration to be alien to those of the letterform (or alien in the context of the words).

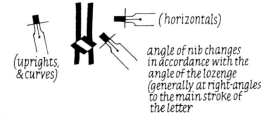

12:3 The same decorative treatment given to one set of capitals

Roman Half-uncials

Bamberg, Staatsbibliothek, Ms. Patr. 87 (B.iv.21), folio 95R. (*Codex Bambergensis*, containing works of Jerome and Augustine.) Written in southern Italy, probably near Naples, during the 6th century. This detail is shown at $3\frac{1}{2}$ times actual size.

Despite the fact that this script is termed 'Half-uncial' it was never directly derived from Uncial hands. Early Uncials developed from scripts such as the *De Bellis Macedonicis* fragment, retaining a slanted, 'natural' pen angle, whereas early Half-uncials, following scripts such as the Livy *Epitome*, were written with a very flat (straight) pen angle (see *Historical Scripts* Introduction). However, Half-uncial hands were later to become the inspiration for minuscule scripts.

This manuscript clearly reveals the insistent flat pen angle of Half-uncial scripts. It is most obviously seen in the vertical strokes (and results in the distortion of weight distribution in the letter **N**), and in most curves. A slight angle of about 10°, however, can be recognised in some curved strokes. A steeper angle is used for the upper strokes of **c**, **f** and long **s**. The 'clubbed' ascenders are probably made with a second stroke overlaying the first. Note the unusually full tail of the **g** (which looks like the numeral 5), the low sweep of the branch of the **r** and the lively **x**.

60

CHAPTER 13

HALF-UNCIALS

This alphabet (here and on the following pages in two versions) has similarities of form to Uncials, though it is not directly derived from them. It has a similar roundness of form, but has achieved a full minuscule status. Both versions here are written with a flat pen angle and would now normally have flat-pen Uncials, or perhaps Versals, as accompanying capitals (though historically a larger size of minuscule was most often used). The two versions have a similar form but with variations of detail.

Roman

If this hand is compared with the next, it can be seen how quite small differences give a distinct change of texture to a passage of text, despite the use of a similar pen angle. Here, the longer ascenders and descenders immediately emphasise the minuscule character despite the remnants of capital letterforms. The simple terminals suggested — they involve a more straightforward pen movement than the club terminals of the historical example (though the latter are not an exaggerated version of their type) — make the letterforms more 'Roman' and therefore more 'modern-looking' than those of the Insular script. The long **s**, archaic **g** and **t**, and an **r** which has barely left

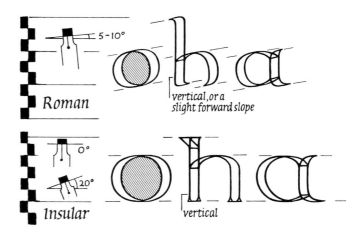

13:1 Two versions of Half-uncials

its capital form are all elements which make us hesitate to accept the historical model visually as a Roman minuscule script. Otherwise it is almost solely the flat-pen quality which gives Half-uncials their character.

Initials were historically of a larger size of the same letter and lines of more importance were written in flat-pen Uncials.

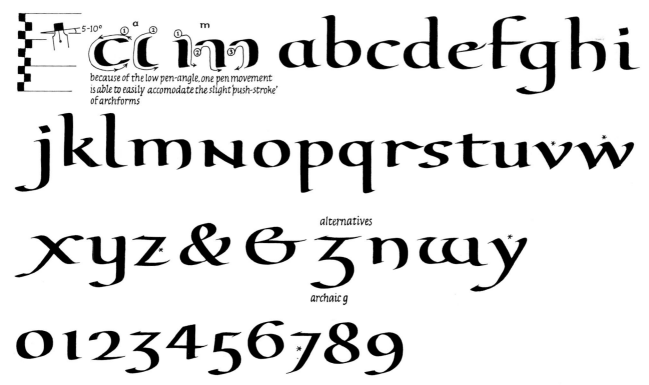

13:2 Roman Half-uncials and numerals

Insular Half-Uncials

Lichfield, Cathedral Library. *The Lichfield (St Chad) Gospels*, page 131 for actual-size details at foot of page. (Three Gospels in Latin, the manuscript now ends at Luke 3:9.) Written, possibly in Wales, between 710 and 720. The book is known to have been at Llandaff by the 8th century. This detail is shown at twice actual size.

Insular Half-uncial scripts were first used in Christian Ireland. Most probably they developed from Italian cursive Half-uncials like those of the 6th century Arator manuscript offset in Oxford (CLA Suppl: 1740). One of the earliest known Irish manuscripts, *Codex Usserianus* in Dublin (CLA2:271), written *c* 600, shows a script which is somewhere between the Italian and the Insular Half-uncial. From Ireland the Insular Half-uncial spread to Anglo-Saxon Northumbria and to other parts of Britain.

The script of the *St Chad Gospels* is not so ponderous as that of the *Lindisfarne Gospels* and it is more confident than that of the *Book of Durrow*, and much more rhythmic than those of the *Book of Kells*. While the greater part of the script is written with a flat pen angle, certain strokes in the letters **c**, **g**, **p**, **r**, **s**, **t** and **x** require a slightly slanted angle, up to about 20° for **g**. Note the heavy wedge serifs done with a second, overlapping stroke of the pen and the use of the corner of the pen to complete strokes on **t** and **x**. Note the upright **d** (other Insular Half-uncial manuscripts use an Uncial form) and the alternative forms of **n**.

Insular

The Insular hand is quite idiosyncratic: the serifs are wedge-shaped; the ascenders and descenders are short; and the archaic **g** is unusual (rather illegible to present-day eyes though its use in particular words may explain its meaning). Other letterforms which contribute to the over-all 'antique' appearance are **f**, the rounded form of **b** and **l**, the Uncial type of **N**, round **t**, **u** and **w**. Other historical examples will suggest that a lighter nib width-to-height ratio give it a closer relationship to Roman forms, and this also would weaken the very particular associations with its places of origin. The serifs to horizontals of the archaic **g**

and **t** involve similar pen manipulation to that of some Uncial characters, but in a reverse direction (**13:3**).

A distinctive rhythm is created by the pattern of round strokes and triangular wedge serifs which are written usually deliberately and probably slowly.

Initials were historically a larger size of the same letter, not from a separate capital alphabet. Larger sizes still were used for titles, introductory lines and so on, perhaps made with a compound construction similar to that of versals. For an even more important occasion, a rectangular version of letters was often used which, although exciting as abstract form, is too illegible for general use today.

13:3 Insular Half-uncials and numerals with details of serif formation

CHAPTER 14

PRE-COPPERPLATE ITALIC SCRIPT

LETRE facile à jmiter pour les femmes.

Nous deuons peser et estimer les biens et faueurs que nous receuons de Dieu, auec nos biens temporels, beaucoup plus que tous les maux qui nous sçauroient aduenir .

Entre les anciens la pauureté ne pouuoit empescher vn homme d'estre juste, sage, et vaillant, et s'abusent ceux qui estiment que sans grands moyens vn homme puisse faire acte vertueux comme si la vertu procedoit de richesse, et le vice de pauureté .

aaabbbcccdddeeeefffgghhiillmmnnooppqqrrssttttvvuuxxyyzz&

14.1 An example of pre-Copperplate Italic writing by Lucas Materot, Avignon, 1608, reproduced from *Penmanship of the Sixteenth, Seventeenth and Eighteenth Centuries* by Louis F. Day (Batsford).

Copperplate scripts became so called because the move away from Formal Italic to script written with a flexible and more pointed quill coincided with the introduction of intaglio printing from a copper plate. The writing masters of the time were not slow to capitalise on this method of reproducing their exemplars. The method was very sympathetic to their mode of writing; indeed, one is tempted to think that the method of engraving with a pointed graver may have influenced the calligraphers. Certainly the turning of the metal plate, supported on a sandbag, against the engraving tool is an excellent way of producing long, fluent curves or flourishes. The earlier writing masters who taught Italic had been comparatively badly served by their engravers on wood.

There was an interim period when a narrower 'broad' pen was being used, with some pressure, to produce a let-terform which is essentially a 'Copperplate' sort of Italic. It has the ligatures, extra slope and one or two typical letterforms. The alphabet illustrated here shows such a letterform. It is written with a fine metal pen and little pressure. It can be considered a variety of Italic, but note how the characteristics mentioned above are sufficient to distinguish the texture of an area of text from the Italics previously illustrated.

Considerable control and deliberate formation are needed because of the delicate pen weight and formal rhythm that this alphabet requires. The cursive appearance is emphasised by emphatic slope, ligatures and loops. This hand is probably less difficult to learn than 'pure' Copperplate which needs familiarity with a totally different technique that relies on pen pressure – which puts it beyond the scope of this book.

14:2 Another example of pre-Copperplate Italic writing by Jarry(?) for Henriette de Coligny's *Triomphe de Amaryllis*, *c*1650 (Victoria and Albert Museum, ms L1056–1950). These two small sections show the obvious use of the broad pen.

14:3 Alphabets and numerals for italic writing in the pre-Copperplate style

CHAPTER 15

NEULAND

ABCDEFGHIJKLMN
OPQRSTUVWXYZ
1234567890

15:1 Neuland typeface 1923

15:2 Alphabet of the Neuland letterform cut by Fritz Kredel or Gustav Eichenauer 1934 for *The Little ABC Book of Rudolf Koch* (David R. Godine)

This is the name of the typeface designed and cut by Rudolf Koch for the Klingspor foundry in 1923. He is said to have designed each size as it was cut, so individual letters vary considerably from one size to another. Students may have been introduced to it in workshops under the name of the typeface, so the name is retained here, although the historical exemplar shows that he also wrote similar letterforms by hand. The typeface demonstrates a sympathy with the technique of cutting away background metal to leave raised letters and it also bears evidence of Koch's consciously manipulative way of using the pen, which is in this case a novel way for its time. A similar kind of free sanserif letter is to be found in German stonecut lettering.

In writing such an alphabet one must bear in mind the natural marks of the pen and the fact that its angle needs to be adjusted continually to produce a sanserif letter with a fairly regular weight of stroke. The fine thins inevitably made by the broad pen held at a constant angle are sacrificed but replaced by another kind of visual interest. The counters vary their shape at the meeting point of strokes because the pen is held at changing angles. The simple nature of these junctions needs to be preserved if the character of this kind of letter is to retain its freshness – it is *not* an attempt to draw a sanserif monoline letter with a tool which does not naturally do that. Simple rules for changing the pen angle need to be adopted so that the method of formation is evident, as in other more formal alphabets made with the broad pen.

Alternatively, for occasional contrast, a constant, flat pen angle can be adopted for letters with curved strokes (see **15:3** for alternatives). This variation introduces the sparkle of a pen stroke tapering to a fine point whilst the form of the curve retains something of the weight of other letters. The mixture of the two forms is very much a question of visual balance in the context of a given text.

The natural chunkiness of the letter offers opportunities for designing closely-packed, dramatic textures of words and for giving the letter-strokes themselves colour and/or texture from the directness with which the strokes are made (perhaps with a wooden pen, or on a textured paper surface). This letter has Germanic associations which need to be taken into account in considering its possible use as text, but it also has possibilities for simplification to a point of semi-abstraction when the forms will lose those associations.

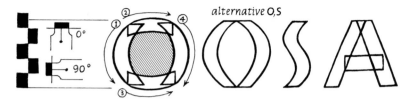

alternative O,S

The two pen angles are respected in principle but slight variations will be observed, due to the freedom of execution.
Variations in proportions are part of the free execution but are due also to the use of alternative forms written with a single pen-angle.
These letters are therefore intended as a guide rather than definitive forms.

ABCDEFGHIJ
KLMNOPQ
RSTUVWXY

alternative letters, single pen-angle (0°)

Z&BCDGJOP
QRSU&;;"!?/
0123456789+

alternative numerals, single pen-angle (0°)

0123456989

15:3 An alphabet of capitals and numerals with similar weight and appearance to those of Neuland. Some alternative letterforms are also offered.

CHAPTER 16

ITALIC FLOURISHES

Because of its cursive qualities, which convey the quickness of the writing, and the resultant slope to the right, Italic is a natural base for flourishes. The simplest form of these is the slight extension of ascenders to the right and of descenders to the left. Coupled with the extra line space needed to avoid collisions of these extensions between the lines, this gives a typical rhythm to text written in cursive Italic. Care is needed lest such extensions overpower the word pattern.

More deliberate and more complex flourishes build on this principle and may extend into margins or larger line spaces. Deliberate may mean deliberately chosen letterforms which can be flourished in a minor, almost casual way; or it may mean a consciously designed pattern of flourishes as a major focal point on the page or as a border surrounding it. In either case, it is very easy to overdo this added decoration which needs to retain a visual relationship with the letters from which it stems. The simplest and often most satisfactory way of achieving this is to make the source of flourishes a physical extension of a convenient letter. Often a minor, thin stroke or a serif extension is a happier starting point than a thick stroke. Although it is a possibility, flourishes as detached units rarely look so satisfactory.

At first it is almost like studying a new alphabet. The lines of extension enclose their own counters as do letters, so it is important that the shapes be sympathetic with the letters they accompany (**16:1**), although they will usually be on a different scale and may overlap and create yet more sub-shapes. If they are round the edge of a piece of calligraphy the whole piece acquires a new outline which needs to be kept under control and which may require fresh attention to the width of final margins.

If a large, sharpened pen is being used, the making of long, continuous lines may be difficult and it may be desirable to make a complex group of flourishes in sections, as though they were enlarged formal letters. This involves pen lifts and pull- rather than push-strokes. If the form of such a group is well thought out in advance, it can be made fairly slowly and deliberately; this may seem like drawing rather than writing but it can still retain the necessary freshness of appearance. Beyond a certain size, wrist or arm, rather than finger, movements may be necessary. These require preparatory 'dummy runs' and a 'follow-through' as though a golf or tennis stroke were being practised.

Flourishes to occupy space between lines may also require some pre-planning of the amount of line space needed and the best departure points. Otherwise there will be 'collisions' of flourishes ascending and descending at the same point. The amount of line space required can be quite surprisingly larger than a 'norm' of, say, double the x height. This is extending the discussion into questions of layout, which is beyond the scope of this book; suffice it to say that a flourish with a generously fluent curve needs space to develop fully.

16:1 Oval-based letters look best with a similar basis for the flourishes, a pointed italic with pointed flourishes, etc.

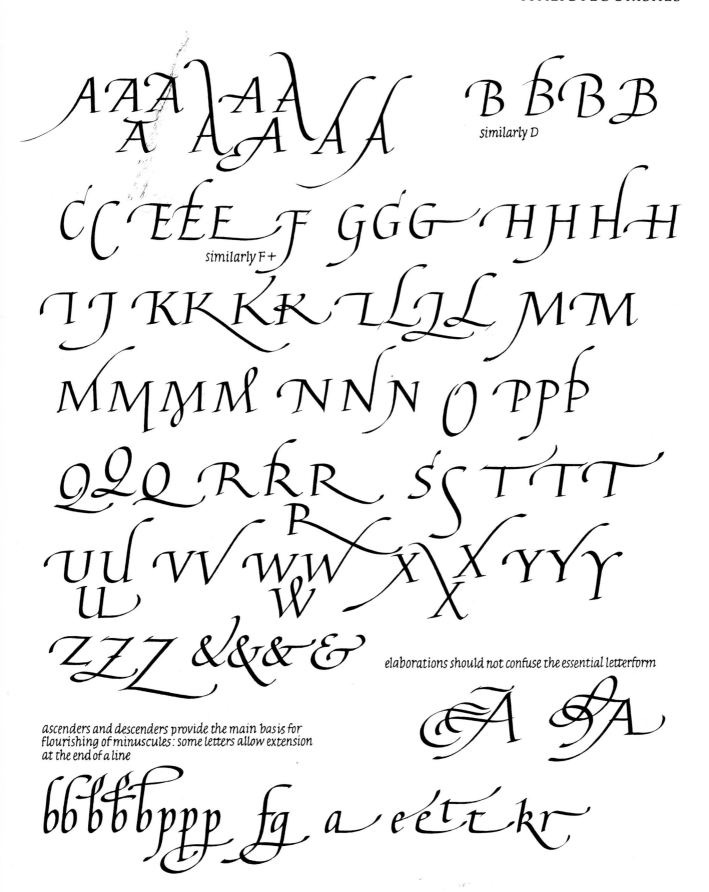

elaborations should not confuse the essential letterform

ascenders and descenders provide the main basis for
flourishing of minuscules: some letters allow extension
at the end of a line

16:2 Possible points of origination for flourishes

16:3 Elaborations from one or more points should not confuse the basic letter structure or legibility and are best kept away from the main letterform.

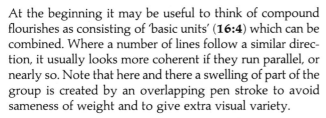

Ann Hechle
A detail from the illustration on page 78. The form of flourish is suggested by the nature of the words as well as by the position of the flourishes in the design.

John Woodcock
A bookplate where flourishes are semi-illustrative and form a link with the drawing.

At the beginning it may be useful to think of compound flourishes as consisting of 'basic units' (**16:4**) which can be combined. Where a number of lines follow a similar direction, it usually looks more coherent if they run parallel, or nearly so. Note that here and there a swelling of part of the group is created by an overlapping pen stroke to avoid sameness of weight and to give extra visual variety.

If flourishes are composed into a cartouche or border, it is helpful to keep in mind imaginary limits. Space is usually desirable round the central word or words. The pen may have to be turned as it travels round the shape so as to avoid conjunctions of heavy strokes that make patches of heaviness. Generally, thick crossing thin is the guide.

Occasionally the free-flowing lines of flourishes may be formed into shapes which reflect in a semi-illustrative way the sense of the words (without matching the worst

excesses of the eighteenth-century writing masters at their most competitive!) Alternatively, in an abstract expressive way, they can build up a texture of flourishes to match the mood of the words, whether it is delicately decorative or strong and aggressive.

As mentioned previously, it is wise not to attempt something too complicated too soon. Be selective about how much (or how little) is required to support the sense of the words. A little goes a long way. The advice about pre-planning seems contrary to the free nature of flourishes, but if the shape to be written is clear in the mind before starting, it is more likely to be fluently written than if sudden changes have to be made halfway; a clear concept can be written with more freedom and confidence than something that is uncertain. This applies to flourishes as much as to letters.

basic units

variations and multiples

1 *sinuous line*

2 *spiral*

3 *'clouds'*

4 *knots/endings*

combinations

1+2

2+3

1+1 *'parallels'+ 'swell'*

1+1+3

1+1+2

etcetera

16:4 Basic units, combinations, multiples, etc.

CHAPTER 17

SPACING OF CAPITALS AND MINUSCULES

Although layout and design problems are not the chief concern of this book, they do obviously affect the overall written form, as does the physical writing position which has already been mentioned, and they cannot be ignored. Immediately one begins to write words rather than individual letters, even for practice, the question of spacing arises. The use of space, indeed, is a prime consideration in designing the layout for calligraphic (or any other) letterforms.

The elements of spacing are letter-, word-, and line-spacing. They all need to be related to the space allowed for margins if there is to be a coherent design which takes into account legibility, readability and the function of the piece of work. Legibility has been defined as the certainty of deciphering; readability may be thought of as ease of reading in particular circumstances. For instance, a poster will have different requirements from those of a small manuscript book of poetry.

Unfortunately, the mass of reading matter to which we are exposed daily is often badly spaced and its influence must be resisted if we are to avoid repeating similar bad habits in our writing. Any newspaper will demonstrate the horrors of word- and line-spacing which arise from the quick typesetting of 'justified' columns (with even margins left and right) in lines too short to allow letter-spaces or word-spaces to become at all regular. Modern typesetting machinery can reduce or increase both kinds of space in order to make words fit a line of particular length. The spacing is consequently too tight or too ample and certainly uneven from line to line. If word-spaces are too wide, there will be 'rivers' of space running down the page and disrupting the movement of the eye along the line; the unevenness of lines produces a jerky eye movement.

Historical examples show that inscriptions and manuscripts were often being produced until the sixth or seventh century AD without the use of word-spacing (or sometimes a minimal use of a centreline dot instead of a space). But these mostly consist of capitals, which by their nature are read as a series of individual forms. Minuscules are usually read more quickly, in letter groups recognisable as typical 'word outlines' (created by the silhouette of ascenders and descenders as well as individual letter shapes). In fact, quick everyday reading will be accomplished by taking in whole groups of words at once. So capitals lend themselves more readily to wide spacing; minuscules widely spaced tend to destroy the word's typical outline.

The line is, therefore, the main unit of design in both cases. A word-space should always be slightly wider than a letter-space and the line space needs to be greater than either, so that there is no encouragement for the eye to travel vertically except at the end of lines. Of course, this applies in the case of passages of text intended for 'normal' reading; there are occasions when the massing of words without line spacing expresses an implicit mood which is more important than simple legibility.

The classic ideal is to have an even amount of space between all letters. As each letter varies in form, this is not as easy as it sounds. Between simple capitals which have a counter closed at each side, the letter-space is easily measurable. Other letterforms have a counter space even though it is not clearly defined and here the final arbiter must be the eye. A simple rule-of-thumb is that two curved strokes will be placed together more closely than two vertical strokes for the areas of letter-space to be even; a mixture of straight and curved will be somewhere in between. On occasion a letter such as **T** may need to overlap the extremities of an adjacent letter such as **A** to achieve a matching letter-space. Combinations of letters such as **TY** and **LA**, will set the lower limit of letter-spaces in areas of formal capitals.

If the character of the text is less formal, such letters may be joined, with some adaptation of the serifs, or be made to overlap if the words make such treatment suitable. In areas of minuscules, combinations of letters such as **ry** and **wy** will tend to leave a 'hole' in an otherwise regular texture of letters unless comparatively wide overall spacing is adopted to allow for them. The danger then is that the whole text may look as though it has consciously added letter-spacing. Alternatively, such combinations can be run together by a simple variation of the serifs or the proportions slightly modified to minimise the appearance in the line of the awkward space between the letters (see the illustrated areas of text in **17:3**). Alphabets of wider or narrower proportions will require spaces appropriate to those proportions.

17:1 shows a way of checking the disparate shapes created by spacing between capitals by comparing them with a

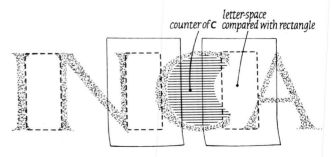

17:1 Using a rectangle drawn on an overlay to check the space between capitals

Letterandwordspacesaffectreadabilityandlegibility

The lack of word-spaces leaves this surprisingly legible – the eye relying on word outlines – until a doubt arises about where 'word' and 'spaces' end and begin; is there another word we have misread?

Letter and word spaces affect readability and legib

There is more than enough word-space in this line. Uneven letter-spacing makes for jerky reading. The sequences of upright strokes are too close for the texture made by the round letters.

Letter and word spaces affe

Widely spaced minuscules make uncomfortable and slow reading; the definition of the word outlines has been lost. We are not used to 'spelling out' any amount of minuscules unless, perhaps, a single word for emphasis.

LETTER AND WORD SPAC

Wide spacing of capitals is acceptable, though slow to read. The word-spaces are sufficient to separate words. There is no word outline to guide the eye, so we are used to spelling out capitals, relying on differences of letter shapes.

LETTER AND WORD SPACES AFFECT READAB

Close letter- and word-spaced capitals are read more quickly; they also look more urgent. If the texture is regular, it is as acceptable as that of the line above, depending on circumstances.

Letter and word spaces affect readability and le

For minuscule text, this is more acceptable than the first three lines. The texture is even; one reads quickly and surely, recognising the outlines of words, or even whole groups of words, at a glance.

17:2 Letter- and word-spaces in single lines

rectangle drawn on an overlay. This is a useful aid to training a discerning eye or in occasional cases of doubt, but it is obviously tedious to rely on this cumbersome procedure and, as soon as possible, the judgement of the eye should become the sole arbiter.

The illustrations on this page and overleaf show the effect of different spacings in single lines of capitals and minuscules and in blocks of text.

Lines of capitals may be quite widely letter-spaced because the limitations of ascenders and descenders do not apply, so long as care is taken to avoid vertical 'rivers' of white space breaking the continuity of the horizontal line.

A usual minimum line space for minuscules is twice the x-height. This will avoid clashes of ascenders and descenders between the lines provided that they are generally slightly shorter than the x-height. If they are longer, say, in the case of Carolingian or an Italic with extended ascenders and descenders, the line space will need to be adjusted accordingly; careful pre-planning can, of course,

avoid any clashes. Wider line spaces than 'normal' may also be used when appropriate to give a sense of airiness, grace and delicacy to a piece.

If we assume that the norm for calligraphic (as distinct from typographic) passages of text is to be 'ranged left' (a regular left-hand margin and a ragged right-hand one), the numbers of words per line will have some bearing on spacing and the emphasis on the line unit. It will have considerable bearing on the shape of the whole passage and its relation to margins, but that is a wider design consideration. For any amount of continuous reading, six words per line are a normal minimum, twelve or thirteen a normal maximum. Longer lines will tend to produce a less ragged right-hand margin, but will require greater line spacing if the eye is to return easily to the beginning of the next line. Very short lines will make a very ragged right-hand edge if word spaces are kept properly even. The introduction of a few carefully-chosen word breaks at the ends of lines will help to make line lengths acceptably even.

73

17:3 Passages of text with varying letter-, word- and line-spaces

The unit of reading a passage of text is the line. If line-spacing seems less than word-spacing, vertical 'rivers' of white space disrupt the movement of the eye along the horizontal line. With the line-space greater than letter- and word-spaces, the eye is helped to read along the line. If there are not too many words in the line, the eye easily jumps to the beginning of the next line.

And in the heat of the furnace will he wrestle with his work: the noise of the hammer will be in his ear, and his eyes upon the pattern of the vessel: he set his heart upon perfecting his works...

a Line-space is the same as the x-height of the lettering. The space between letters is normal, but the spaces between words are too big. This emphasises vertical white shapes in the overall texture of the writing and disrupts the line as a unit.

And in the heat of the furnace will he wrestle with his work: the noise of the hammer will be in his ear, and his eyes upon the pattern of the vessel: he set his heart upon perfecting his works...

b Line- and word-spacing are the same as **a** but letter-spacing is wider. This disguises word-spacing but does not affect the vertical disruption of lines.

And in the heat of the furnace will he wrestle with his work: the noise of the hammer will be in his ear, and his eyes upon the pattern of the vessel: he set his heart upon perfecting his works...

c Line- and word-spacing are the same as **a** but the space between letters is tighter (too close for a regular texture of writing). This also emphasises the word-spaces.

And in the heat of the furnace will he wrestle with his work: the noise of the hammer will be in his ear, and his eyes upon the pattern of the vessel: he set his heart upon perfecting his works...

d Word- and letter-spacing are the same as **a** but line-spacing is one and a half times the x-height. This disguises the too-wide word-spaces but does not cancel their vertical disruption of the lines.

And in the heat of the furnace will he wrestle with with his work: the noise of the hammer will be in his ear, and his eyes upon the pattern of the vessel: he set his heart upon perfecting his works...

e Close letter- and word-spacing. Line-spacing is the same as the x-height. This emphasises the line as a horizontal unit despite the close line-spacing.

And in the heat of the furnace will he wrestle with his work: the noise of the hammer will be in his ear, and his eyes upon the pattern of the vessel: he set his heart upon perfecting his works...

f Close letter- and word-spacing, as in **e**. Line-space is twice the x-height. This increases the emphasis of the horizontal lines. Note length of lines in comparison with **a** and **b**.

And in the heat of the furnace will he wrestle with his work: the noise of the hammer will be in his ear, and his eyes upon the pattern of the vessel: he set his heart upon perfecting his work...

g Line-spacing is the same as **f** (twice the x-height). Letter- and word-spacing are slightly increased but emphasis is still on the horizontal lines.

And in the heat of the furnace will he wrestle with his work: the noise of the hammer will be in his ear, and his eyes upon the pattern of the vessel: he set his heart upon perfecting his work...

h In this example, more words per line give extra emphasis to horizontals.

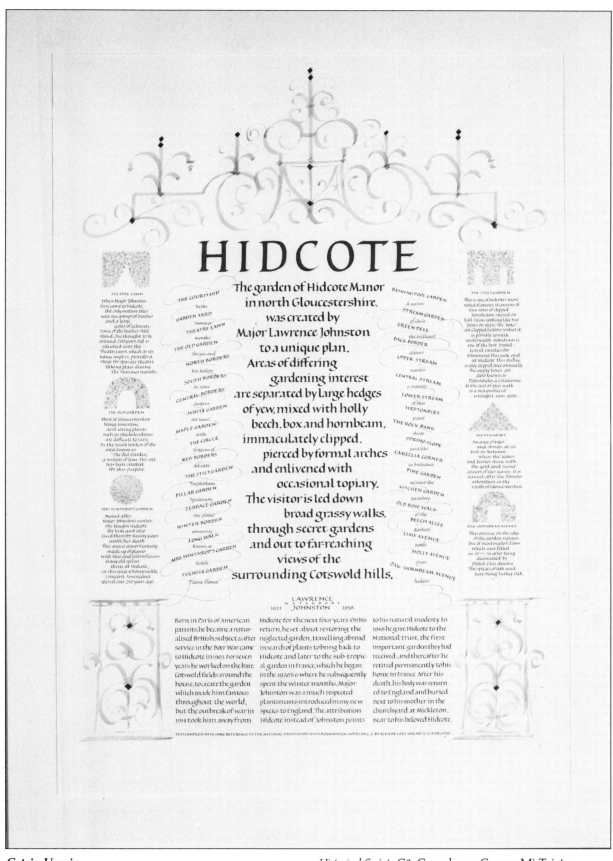

HIDCOTE

The garden of Hidcote Manor in north Gloucestershire, was created by Major Lawrence Johnston to a unique plan. Areas of differing gardening interest are separated by large hedges of yew, mixed with holly beech, box and hornbeam, immaculately clipped, pierced by formal arches and enlivened with occasional topiary. The visitor is led down broad grassy walks, through secret gardens and out to far-reaching views of the surrounding Cotswold hills.

LAWRENCE
WATERBURY
1871 · JOHNSTON · 1958

Born in Paris of American parents he became a naturalised British subject & after service in the Boer War came to Hidcote in 1907. For seven years he worked on the bare Cotswold fields around the house, to create the garden which made him famous throughout the world, but the outbreak of war in 1914 took him away from Hidcote for the next four years. On his return, he set about restoring the neglected garden, travelling abroad in search of plants to bring back to Hidcote and later to the sub-tropical garden in France, which he began in the 1920s & where he subsequently spent the winter months. Major Johnston was a much respected plantsman & introduced many new species to England. The attribution Hidcote instead of Johnston points to his natural modesty. In 1948 he gave Hidcote to the National Trust, the first important garden they had received, and thereafter he retired permanently to his home in France. After his death, his body was returned to England and buried next to his mother in the churchyard at Mickleton, near to his beloved Hidcote.

TEXT COMPILED WITH SOME REFERENCE TO THE NATIONAL TRUST GUIDE WITH BIOGRAPHICAL NOTES ON L.J. BY ALVILDE LEES-MILNE/C.U. MARCH '90

Catrin Unwin
Hidcote. The text written in a hand based on that of the Cnut Charter, a compressed English minuscule, cf.

Historical Scripts C8. Gouache on Canson Mi-Teintes paper. 35″ × 27 3/16″ (89 × 60 cm) 1990 (National Trust collection)

75

CHAPTER 18

DIFFERENT PEN WEIGHTS

Each alphabet illustrated has been introduced by an example of the suggested nib width-to-x-height ratio. This is partly to preserve a direct relationship with the historical ancestor which gave it its individual quality and partly to emphasise distinctions (as in the case of the varieties of roman minuscule) for the purposes of study. However, once a degree of confidence has been achieved, the way is open to experiment with variations of weight and form, but weights are simpler to begin with. Such

experiment extends the calligrapher's repertoire vastly. The desire for variation will usually arise from the design requirements of the particular piece of work in hand, one of which may well be the usefulness of an element of contrast.

For reasons of space, this page concentrates on one type of italic as it is a letterform which allows a full range of variations; some alphabets have less potential.

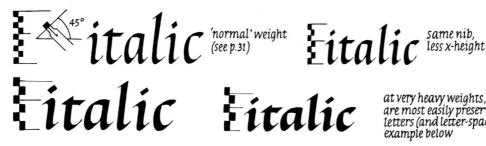

45° *italic* 'normal' weight (see p.31)   *italic* same nib, less x-height

italic   **italic** at very heavy weights, counters and branching archforms are most easily preserved by widening the proportions of letters (and letter-spacing in sympathy), but see last example below

italic light, average width

at light weights the width-to-height ratio of the basic elliptical o can be varied easily, without problems of the weight of stroke intruding on counter or branching of the archform

italic narrow   *italic* wide

italic light weight, narrow proportions, short ascenders

o italic   **italic**

different skeleton forms/weights

o italic   *italic*

italic narrow, heavy weight, close letter-spacing: to preserve the branching the archforms become more pointed

18:1 Effect of different pen weights on italic

Obviously, skeleton roman capitals and minuscules soon take on the character of slanted-pen letters if their weight is much increased. Not that the labels matter; they are merely varieties for the purpose of study. Letterforms may demand variation of construction if their character is to survive significant increase in weight. For instance, very heavy weights of roman capitals will demand changes of pen angle and/or manipulation, as well as proportion, if some of their counters and the relationship

of thick to thin are to survive the general increase of weight in the weight-to-height ratio (see **18:2**). Textura loses a great deal of its typical character if much reduced in weight. For a particular occasion, an alternative technique is to write with a double-outline pen which will keep something of the boldness of proportion whilst reducing the blackness on the page. Judgement is required, then, in making use of the vast potential of weight variations.

30° pen-angle, 'normal'
Roman proportions

letters whose skeleton
form is divided horizontally
give the greatest constraints
to increasing their weight

30° pen angle

flatter pen-angle desirable
(about 20°), otherwise
counters look too small
compared with weight of the
horizontals: for the same
reason proportions are
widened: some manipulation
of the pen, especially for serifs

letter widths increased even more
for the same reason as in the previous
example: considerable manipulation
of pen-angle/corner of nib for serifs
and thin strokes of **s**

the naturally angular quality of Textura increases
with extra weight – its letters' width merely needs
to be increased to preserve counters:
lightening its weight lessens the angularity unless
the letters are compressed in width

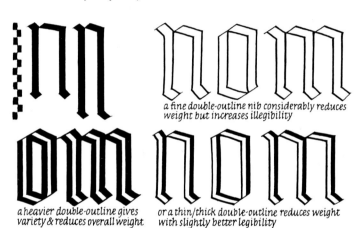

a fine double-outline nib considerably reduces
weight but increases illegibility

a heavier double-outline gives
variety & reduces overall weight

or a thin/thick double-outline reduces weight
with slightly better legibility

18:2 Variety of examples with
different pen weights

weight | width | slope
weight | width | slope
skeleton form · letter-spacing

18:3 The variables

Ann Hechle

Lavender's Blue. One of a series. Varied italic minuscules with flourishes and compound capitals. Grey, blue and light green on vellum. The central cross in shell gold and burnished gold on gesso. 11″ × 8″ (28 × 20.5 cm) inside frame. 1988
(Author's collection)

Tom Perkins
Bookjacket for Golgonooza Press. Pointed Italic
minuscules and Italic capitals. Printed in dark red and dark
grey on buff paper. Front cover 9″ × 6½ (23 × 16.5 cm)
1990

BOOKS

J. J. G. Alexander, *The Decorated Letter* (Thames & Hudson
1978)

Kathryn A. Atkins, *Masters of the Italic Letter* (Allen Lane,
The Penguin Press 1988)

Janet Backhouse, *The Illuminated Manuscript* (Phaidon 1979)

Ann Camp, *Pen Lettering* (A & C Black 1984)

Heather Child, *Calligraphy Today: twentieth century tradition
and practice* (A & C Black 1988)

Heather Child, ed., *Edward Johnston: Formal Penmanship and
Other Papers* (Lund Humphries 1971)

Heather Child, ed., *The Calligrapher's Handbook* (A & C
Black 1985)

Heather Child and Justin Howes, eds. *Edward Johnston:
Lessons in Formal Writing* (Lund Humphries 1986)

Heather Child, Heather Collins, Ann Hechle and Donald
Jackson, eds, *More than Fine Writing – Irene Wellington:
Calligrapher (1904–84)* (Pelham 1986)

*Contemporary Calligraphy: Modern Scribes and Lettering Artists
II* (Trefoil 1986)

David Diringer, *Writing* (1962)

Alfred Fairbank, *A Book of Scripts* (Penguin 1962)

Nicolete Gray, *Lettering as Drawing* (Oxford University
Press 1971)

Nicolete Gray, *A History of Lettering* (Phaidon 1986)

Susanne Haines, *The Calligrapher's Project Book* (Collins
1987)

Peter Halliday, ed., *Calligraphy Masterclass* (Collins 1990)

Michael Harvey, *Creative Lettering* (Bodley Head 1985)

Humanistic Script of the 15th and 16th Centuries (Bodleian
Picture Book, no. 12, 1960)

Donald Jackson, *The Story of Writing* (Studio Vista 1981,
now Trefoil)

Edward Johnston, *Writing and Illuminating, and Lettering*
(originally published 1906, now A & C Black)

Stan Knight, *Historical Scripts* (A & C Black 1984)

Hans E. Meyer, *Development of Writing* (Stampfli Zurich
1977)

A. S. Osley and Berthold Wolpe, *Scribes and Sources* (Faber
& Faber 1980)

Charles Pearce, *The Anatomy of Letters* (Taplinger New York
1987)

Jan Tschichold, *An Illustrated History of Writing and Lettering*
(Zwemmer 1946)

Joyce Irene Whalley, *The Pen's Excellencie: A Pictorial History
of Western Calligraphy* (paperback edition, Taplinger
New York 1980)

PERIODICALS

The Scribe, journal of the Society of Scribes and Illuminators
(54 Boileau Road, London SW13 9BL, UK)

Calligraphy Review (1624 24th Avenue SW, Norman OK
73072, USA)

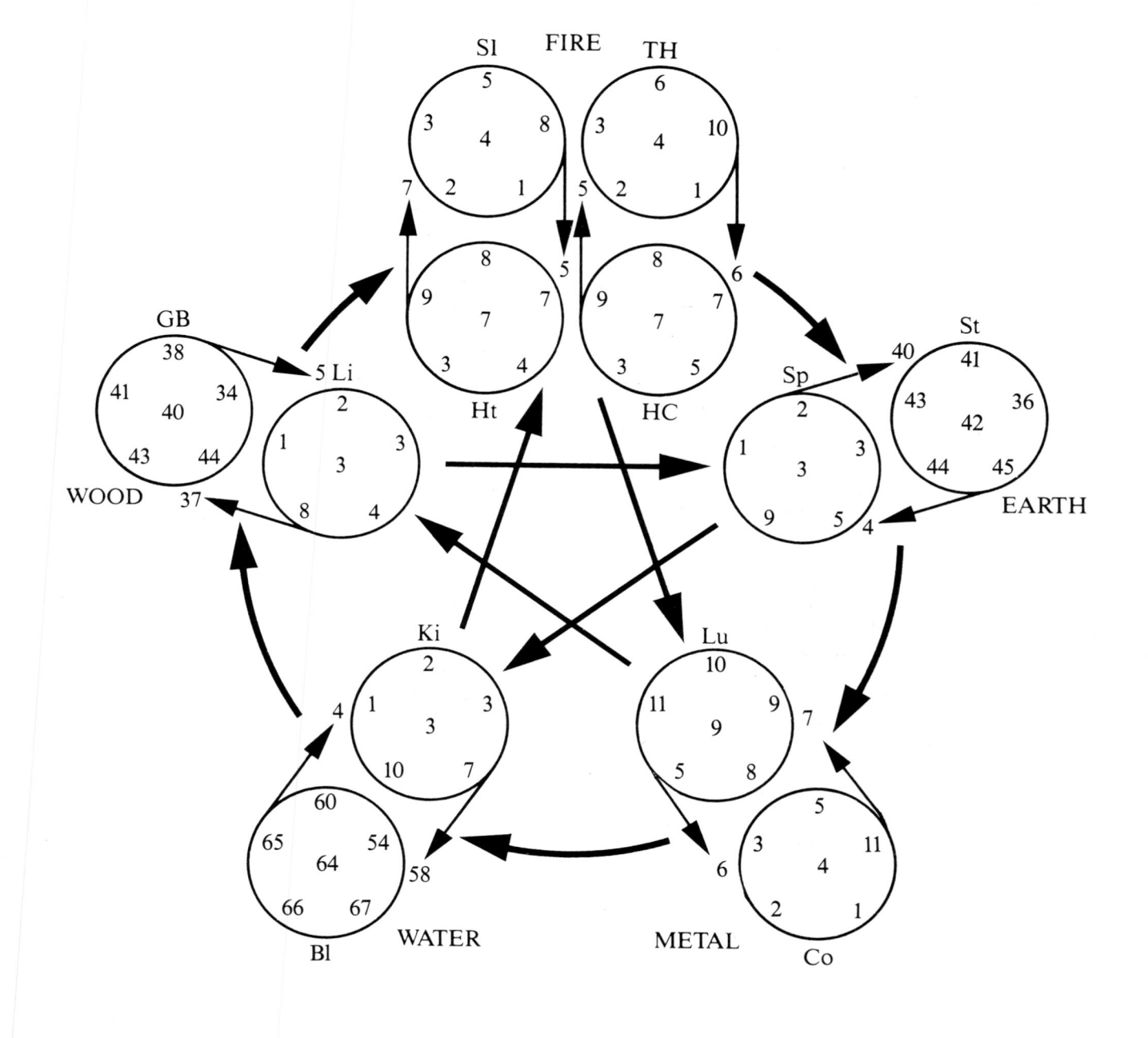

THE FIVE TRANSFORMATIONS

The Chinese Clock

Meridian	Hours	Horary Point
Lu	03-05	Lu8
Co	05-07	Co1
St	07-09	St36
Sp	09-11	Sp3
Ht	11-13	Ht8
SI	13-15	SI5
Bl	15-17	Bl66
Ki	17-19	Ki10
HC	19-21	HC8
TH	21-23	TH6
GB	23-01	GB41
Li	01-03	Li1

Law of Mid-Day/Mid-Night:

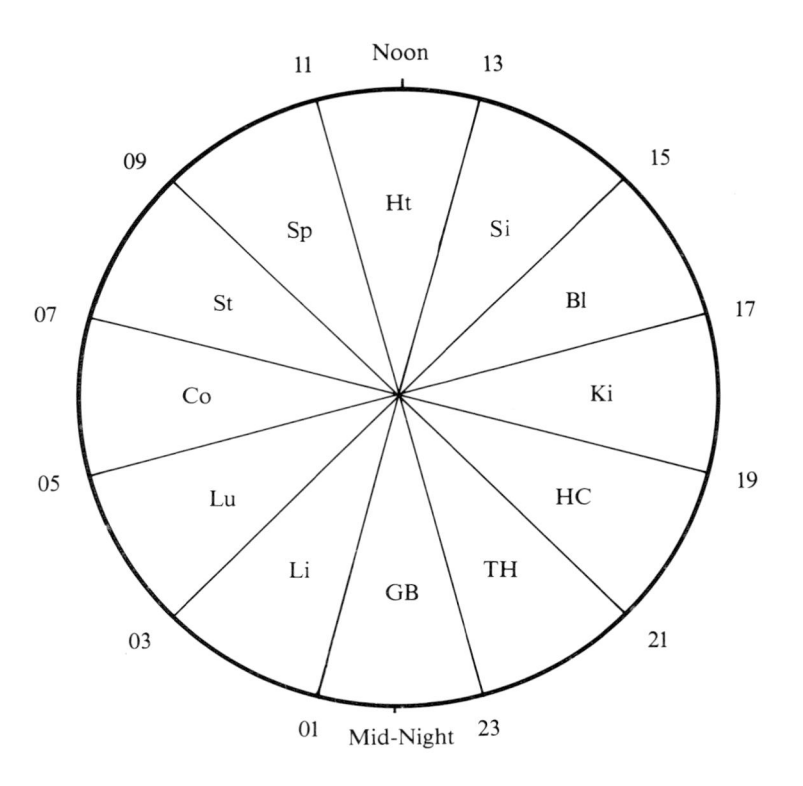

'An action taken on one organ will have an opposite action on the organ diametrically opposite it.' The action is strongest if a Yin organ is stimulated in a Yin time (12-24 hours) and a Yang organ in a Yang time (24-12 hours).

In practice it is found that only strong stimulation calls the Law into effect — if an organ is given only moderate stimulation, then that organ alone is affected. Also in practice, the energies do tend to equalize themselves, i.e. by tonifying the Sp in the afternoon the TH would be sedated, but if the TH were already in a depleted state, then tonification of the Sp would tend to reinforce it and bring both Sp and TH to a more balanced condition.

INDEX OF POINTS IN PINYIN

Shidou	Sp17	Wailing	St26	Yangxi	Co5
Shiguan	Ki18	Waiqiu	GB36	Yaoshu	GV2
Shimen	CV5	Wangu (Hand)	SI4	Yaoyangguan	GV3
Shousanli	Co10	Wangu (Head)	GB12	Yemen	TH2
Shuaigu	GB8	Weicang	Bl45	Yifeng	TH17
Shufu	Ki27	Weidao	GB28	Yinbai	Sp1
Shugu	Bl65	Weishu	Bl21	Yinbao	Li9
Shuidao	St28	Weiyang	Bl53	Yindu	Ki19
Shuifen	CV9	Weizhong	Bl54	Yingchuang	St16
Shuiquan	Ki5	Wenliu	Co7	Yingu	Ki10
Shuitu	St10	Wuchu	Bl5	Yingxiang	Co20
Sibai	St2	Wuli	Co13	Yinjiao (Abdomen)	CV7
Sidu	TH9	Wushu	GB27	Yinjiao (Mouth)	GV28
Siman	Ki14	Wuyi	St15	Yinlian	Li11
Sizhukong	TH23			Yinlingquan	Sp9
Suliao	GV25	Xiabai	Lu4	Yinmen	Bl51
		Xiaguan	St7	Yinshi	St33
Taibai	Sp3	Xiajuxu	St39	Yinxi	Ht6
Taichong	Li3	Xialian	Co8	Yishe	Bl44
Taixi	Ki3	Xialiao	Bl34	Yixi	Bl39
Taiyi	St23	Xiangu	St43	Yongquan	Ki1
Taiyuan	Lu9	Xiaochangshu	Bl27	Youmen	Ki21
Taodao	GV13	Xiaohai	SI8	Yuanye	GB22
Tianchi	HC1	Xiaoluo	TH12	Yuji	Lu10
Tianchong	GB9	Xiawan	CV10	Yunmen	Lu2
Tianchuang	SI16	Xiaxi	GB43	Yutang	CV18
Tianding	Co17	Xiguan	Li7	Yuzhen	Bl9
Tianfu	Lu3	Ximen	HC4	Yuzhong	Ki26
Tianjing	TH10	Xingjian	Li2		
Tianliao	TH15	Xinhui	GV22	Zanzhu	Bl2
Tianquan	HC2	Xinshu	Bl15	Zhangmen	Li13
Tianrong	SI17	Xiongxiang	Sp19	Zhaohai	Ki6
Tianshu	St25	Xiyangguan	GB33	Zhejin	GB23
Tiantu	CV22	Xuanji	CV21	Zhengying	GB17
Tianxi	Sp18	Xuanli	GB6	Zhibian	Bl49
Tianyou	TH16	Xuanlu	GB5	Zhigou	TH6
Tianzhu	Bl10	Xuanshu	GV5	Zhishi	Bl47
Tianzong	SI11	Xuanzhong	GB39	Zhiyang	GV9
Tiaokou	St38	Xuehai	Sp10	Zhiyin	Bl67
Tinggong	SI19			Zhizheng	SI7
Tinghui	GB2	Yamen	GV15	Zhongchong	HC9
Tonggu (Abdomen)	Ki20	Yangbai	GB14	Zhongdu (Leg)	GB32
Tonggu (Foot)	Bl66	Yangchi	TH4	Zhongdu (Foot)	Li6
Tongli	Ht5	Yangfu	GB38	Zhongfeng	Li4
Tongtian	Bl7	Yanggang	Bl43	Zhongfu	Lu1
Tongziliao	GB1	Yanggu	SI5	Zhongji	CV3
Touwei	St8	Yangjiao	GB35	Zhongliao	Bl33
		Yanglao	SI6	Zhonglüshu	Bl29
Waiguan	TH5	Yanglingquan	GB34	Zhongshu	GV7

Zhongting	CV16	Zhongzhu (Hand)	TH3	Zhubin	Ki9
Zhongwan	CV12	Zhouliao	Co12	Zigong	CV19
Zhongzhu (Abdomen)	Ki15	Zhourong	Sp20	Zusanli	St36

INDEX OF POINTS IN WADE-GILES

Chungfeng	Li4	Hsialien	Co8	Kungtsui	Lu6
Chungfu	Lu1	Hsiawan	CV10	Kunlun	Bl60
Chungliao	Bl33	Hsiaochangshu	Bl27		
Chunglushu	Bl29	Hsiaohai	SI8	Laokung	HC8
Chungmen	Sp12	Hsiaolo	TH12	Liangchiu	St34
Chungshu	GV7	Hsiapai	Lu4	Liangmen	St21
Chungting	CV16	Hsienku	St43	Liehchueh	Lu7
Chungtu (GB)	GB32	Hsikuan	Li7	Lienchuan	CV23
Chungtu (Li)	Li6	Hsimen	HC4	Likou	Li5
Chungwan	CV12	Hsingchien	Li2	Linchi	GB15
Chungyang	St42	Hsinshu	Bl15	Linghsu	Ki24
Chupin	Ki9	Hsinhui	GV22	Lingtai	GV10
Ch'upin	GB7	Hsiunghsiang	Sp19	Lingtao	Ht4
Chutse	HC3	Hsiyangkuan	GB33	Litui	St45
Chuyuan	SI13	Hsuanchi	CV21	Lochueh	Bl8
		Hsuanchung	GB39	Louku	Sp7
		Hsuanli	GB6	Luhsi	TH19
Erhchien	Co2	Hsuanlu	GB5		
Erhmen	TH21	Hsuanshu	GV5	Meichung	Bl3
		Hsuehhai	Sp10	Mingmen	GV4
Feishu	Bl13	Huajoumen	St24	Muchuang	GB16
Feiyang	Bl58	Huakai	CV20		
Fengchih	GB20	Huangmen	Bl46	Naohu	GV17
Fengfu	GV16	Huangshu	Ki16	Naohui	TH13
Fenglung	St40	Huantiao	GB30	Naokung	GB19
Fengmen	Bl12	Huitsung	TH7	Naoshu	SI10
Fengshih	GB31	Huiyang	Bl35	Neikuan	HC6
Fuai	Sp16	Huijin	CV1	Neiting	St44
Fuchieh	Sp14	Hunmen	Bl42		
Fufen	Bl36			Paihuanshu	Bl30
Fuhsi	Bl52			Paihui	GV20
Fuliu	Ki7	Janku	Ki2	Pangkuangshu	Bl28
Fupai	GB10	Jenchung	GV26	Paohuang	Bl48
Fushe	Sp13	Jenying	St9	Penshen	GB13
Futu (St)	St32	Jihyueh	GB24	Pienli	Co6
Futu (Co)	Co18	Juchung	St17	Pikuan	St31
Fuyang	Bl59	Juken	St18	Pinao	Co14
				Pingfeng	SI12
Hanyen	GB4	Kanshu	Bl18	Pishu	Bl20
Hengku	Ki11	Kaohuang	Bl38	Pohu	Bl37
Hoku	Co4	Kekuan	Bl41	Pujung	St19
Holiao (Co)	Co19	Keshu	Bl17	Pulang	Ki22
Holiao (TH)	TH22	Kuanchung	TH1	Pushen	Bl61
Houhsi	SI3	Kuangming	GB37		
Houting	GV19	Kuanmen	St22		
Hoyang	Bl55	Kuanyuan	CV4	Sanchiaoshu	Bl22
Hsiachuhsu	St39	Kuanyuanshu	Bl26	Sanchien	Co3
Hsiahsi	GB43	Kufang	St14	Sanli	Co10
Hsiakuan	St7	Kuilai	St29	Sanyanglo	TH8
Hsialiao	Bl34	Kungsun	Sp4	Sanyinchiao	Sp6

Shanchung	CV17	Taihsi	Ki3	Waichiu	GB36
Shangchui	Sp5	Taimo	GB26	Waikuan	TH5
Shangchu	Ki17	Taipai	Sp3	Wailing	St26
Shangchuhsu	St37	Taiyi	St23	Wanku (GB)	GB12
Shanghsing	GV23	Taiyuan	Lu9	Wanku (Si)	SI4
Shangkuan	GB3	Taling	HC7	Weichung	Bl54
Shangliao	Bl31	Tanshu	Bl19	Weishu	Bl21
Shanglien	Co9	Taotao	GV13	Weitao	GB28
Shangwan	CV13	Tapao	Sp21	Weitsang	Bl45
Shangyang	Co1	Tatu	Sp2	Weiyang	Bl53
Shaochung	Ht9	Tatun	Li1	Wenliu	Co7
Shaofu	Ht8	Taying	St5	Wuchu	Bl5
Shaohai	Ht3	Tiaokou	St38	Wuli (Thigh)	Li10
Shaoshang	Lu11	Tichi	Sp8	Wuli (Arm)	Co13
Shaotse	SI1	Tienchih	HC1	Wushu	GB27
Shenchu	GV12	Tienching	TH10	Wuyi	St15
Shenchueh	CV8	Tienchu	Bl10		
Shenfeng	Ki23	Tienchung	GB9	Yamen	GV15
Shenmen	Ht7	Tienchuan	HC2	Yangchiao	GB35
Shenmo	Bl62	Tienchuang	SI16	Yangchih	TH4
Shenshu	Bl23	Tienfu	Lu3	Yangfu	GB38
Shentang	Bl39	Tienhsi	Sp18	Yanghsi	Co5
Shentao	GV11	Tienjung	SI17	Yangkang	Bl43
Shenting	GV24	Tienliao	TH15	Yangku	SI5
Shentsang	Ki25	Tienshu	St25	Yangkuan	GV3
Shihkuan	Ki18	Tienting	Co17	Yanglao	SI6
Shihmen	CV5	Tientsung	SI11	Yanglingchuan	GB34
Shihtou	Sp17	Tientu	CV22	Yangpai	GB14
Shuaiku	GB8	Tienyu	TH16	Yaoshu	GV2
Shufu	Ki27	Tinghui	GB2	Yemen	TH2
Shuichuan	Ki5	Tingkung	SI19	Yifeng	TH17
Shuifen	CV9	Titsang	St4	Yihsi	Bl40
Shuitao	St28	Tiwuhui	GB42	Yinchiao (Jen Mo)	CV7
Shuitu	St10	Touwei	St8	Yinchiao (Tu Mo)	GV28
Shuku	Bl65	Tsanchu	Bl2	Yingchuang	St16
Ssuchukung	TH23	Tsuchiaoyin	GB44	Yinghsiang	Co20
Suliao	GV25	Tsulinchi	GB41	Yinhsi	Ht6
Szuman	Ki14	Tsusanli	St36	Yinku	Ki10
Szupai	St2	Tuituan	GB27	Yinlien	Li11
Szutu	TH9	Tungku (Bl)	Bl66	Yinlingchuan	Sp9
		Tungku (Ki)	Ki20	Yinmen	Bl51
Tachangshu	Bl25	Tungli	Ht5	Yinpai	Sp1
Tachui	GV14	Tungtien	Bl7	Yinpao	Li9
Tachu	Bl11	Tungtzuliao	GB1	Yinshih	St33
Tachü	St27	Tupi	St35	Yintu	Ki19
Tachung	Ki4	Tushu	Bl16	Yishe	Bl44
Taheh	Ki12	Tzukung	CV19	Yuanyeh	GB22
Taheng	Sp15	Tzuliao	Bl32	Yuchen	Bl9
Taichung	Li3			Yuchi	Lu10

Yuchung
Yumen

Ki26
Ki21
Yungchuan
Yumen

Ki1
Lu2
Yutang

Yutang

CV18

TO EVERY THING T
THERE IS A SEASON
AND A TIME TO EV
PURPOSE UNDER
THE HEAVEN. A TIM
1

To every thing there is a
season and a time to ev
purpose under the heav
A time to be born and a
time to die; a time to pla
2

TO EVERY THING TH
IS A SEASON AND A TI
TO EVERY PURPOSE I
UNDER THE HEAVEI
A TIME TO BE BORN /
3

To every thing there is a
season and a time to eve
purpose under the heav
A time to be born, and a t
to die; a time to plant an
4

To every thing there is a:
season and a time to ever
purpose under the heav
A time to be born, and a t
to die; a time to plant an
5

To every thing there is a sea
and a time to every purpos
under the heaven. A time to
be born and a time to die; a
time to plant, and a time to p
6

To every thing there is a season a
a time to every purpose under t
heaven. A time to be born, and
a time to die; a time to plant, a
a time to pluck up that which is
7

To every thing there is a seas
and a time to every purpose
under the heaven. A time to
be born and a time to die; a ti
to plant, and a time to pluck
8

To every thing there is a season a
a time to every purpose under tl
heaven. A time to be born, and a
time to die; a time to plant and
a time to pluck up that which is
9

THE 'BASIC
REPERTOIRE'